PRAISE FOR

The Interpretive Lexicon of Old Testament Hebrew and Aramaic

"This is one of the best, concise, ɛ  task of Hebrew exegesis. In additio information presented in this vol provided summaries and locatio vital to exegetical analysis. I will rᴇ....ᴇ ᴛʜɪs book in all my exegesis courses."

> —**Miles V. Van Pelt,** Alan Hayes Belcher, Jr. Professor of Old Testament and Biblical Languages, Reformed Theological Seminary, Jackson

"The six parts of speech covered in this handy little *vademe-cum* are mostly classifiable as 'minor parts of speech' or 'closed classes,' but they are essential for the proper functioning of the biblical text. Or of any text, since in English, for example, the fifty most common words are all of this sort. Hardly ever does a single rendering or definition do justice to a biblical term, and in this respect the *Lexicon* will especially prove its worth by opening up the possibilities that have to be weighed in the act of translating. By combing through representative dictionaries and grammars and listing and summarising the relevant entries, Gibson and Simon have done a lot of the heavy lifting for the student whose progress to date will typically have concentrated on the construal of verbs and nouns. An additionally useful feature is the treatment of both Old Testament languages—Hebrew and Aramaic—in the one volume."

> —**Robert P. Gordon,** Emeritus Regius Professor of Hebrew, University of Cambridge

"As in most languages, it is the 'little words' that most strongly resist simple glossing. They require careful study. A good lexicon will collect all the uses of each word into one place; but even good lexicons do not consistently supply the syntactical analysis that careful study demands. A good Hebrew/Aramaic grammar will treat the syntax of 'little words'; but when a word fulfils the role of two or more different parts of speech, locating its treatments in a grammar can be time-consuming. Neither do lexica or grammars always agree on the meaning and function of these words. Collecting all the relevant information for 194 Hebrew and 88 Aramaic 'little words' is a stroke of inspiration for which we owe the authors a debt of gratitude. Here, then, is a compendium that belongs in every serious biblical studies library. It promises countless hours of saved labor for students of the Hebrew/Aramaic Scriptures, and a careful curation of scholarly opinion that will empower exegetes to make informed choices."

—**Andrew G. Shead,** head of Old Testament and
Hebrew, Moore Theological College, Sydney

"Gibson and Simon have succeeded in providing 'students, pastors, and scholars with a one-stop guide for the syntactic function and semantic range of all adverbs, conjunctions, interjections, particles, prepositions, and pronouns in the Hebrew and Aramaic Scriptures.' Not only do the entries provide concise summaries of the authors' take on the syntax and semantics of the lexemes covered, but they also provide the reader with summaries of the major dictionaries and grammars as well as cross-references for those who want more detail. I will use this volume with students in my Hebrew exegesis course and my Hebrew readings courses."

—**Mark D. Futato,** Robert L. Maclellan
Professor of Old Testament, Reformed
Theological Seminary, Orlando

AN INTERPRETIVE LEXICON OF

OLD TESTAMENT

HEBREW AND ARAMAIC

AN INTERPRETIVE LEXICON OF

OLD TESTAMENT

HEBREW AND

ARAMAIC

ANALYSIS OF ADVERBS, CONJUNCTIONS,
INTERJECTIONS, PARTICLES,
PREPOSITIONS, AND PRONOUNS

JONATHAN GIBSON
BRYCE SIMON

**ZONDERVAN
ACADEMIC**

ZONDERVAN ACADEMIC

An Interpretive Lexicon of Old Testament Hebrew and Aramaic

Published in Grand Rapids, Michigan, by Zondervan. Zondervan is a registered trademark of The Zondervan Corporation, L.L.C., a wholly owned subsidiary of HarperCollins Christian Publishing, Inc.

Requests for information should be addressed to customercare@harpercollins.com.

Zondervan titles may be purchased in bulk for educational, business, fundraising, or sales promotional use. For information, please email SpecialMarkets@Zondervan .com.

Library of Congress Cataloging-in-Publication Data

Names: Gibson, Jonathan, 1977- author. | Simon, Bryce, 1990- author.
Title: An interpretive lexicon of Old Testament Hebrew and Aramaic : analysis of
    adverbs, conjunctions, interjections, particles, prepositions, and pronouns /
    Jonathan Gibson and Bryce Simon.
Description: Grand Rapids : Zondervan Academic, 2024.
Identifiers: LCCN 2023049671 | ISBN 9780310160502 (paperback)
Subjects: LCSH: Hebrew language--Parts of speech--Glossaries, vocabularies, etc.
    | Aramaic language--Parts of speech--Glossaries, vocabularies, etc. | Bible.
    Old Testament--Language, style. | BISAC: RELIGION / Biblical Reference
    / Language Study | RELIGION / Biblical Criticism & Interpretation / Old
    Testament | LCGFT: Dictionaries.
Classification: LCC PJ4845 .G47 2024 | DDC 492.482/421--dc23/eng/20240201
LC record available at https://lccn.loc.gov/2023049671

Cover design: Tammy Johnson
Interior design: Kait Lamphere

For
Libbie Groves

Beloved colleague,
esteemed teacher extraordinaire

CONTENTS

DETAILED TABLE
OF CONTENTS

xii

PREFACE

This interpretive *Lexicon* is compiled to provide students, pastors, and scholars with a one-stop guide for the syntactic function and semantic range of all adverbs, conjunctions, interjections, particles, prepositions, and pronouns in the Hebrew and Aramaic Scriptures. The *Lexicon* provides a taxonomy of syntactic functions for keywords across the main Hebrew and Aramaic lexicons and grammars. All entries are given page numbers and section references so that they can be conveniently researched in print and digital formats. Functioning both as a lexicon and an interpretive handbook, this resource helps the user quickly and easily determine the range of translation possibilities for a variety of Hebrew and Aramaic terms. It also serves to help the reader of the Old Testament Scriptures move beyond a gloss translation to careful interpretation culminating in a more accurate (re)translation.

We are grateful to Nancy Erickson for her faith in this project and her determination to see it published for the church and the academy. Our thanks to Miles Van Pelt and Gregory Beale for their encouragement in the early stages of the work. Lee Fields provided excellent editorial feedback to help bring the manuscript to its current form. We also wish to thank Aaron Savage for his input and careful editorial checking of an earlier draft of this manuscript.

Finally, this *Lexicon* is dedicated to Libbie Groves, a beloved colleague and esteemed teacher extraordinaire, in honor of her many years of faithful and fruitful service at Westminster Theological Seminary, Philadelphia.

Jonathan Gibson and Bryce Simon
Glenside, Summer 2023, *Soli Deo Gloria*

ABBREVIATIONS

While this *Lexicon* is designed to be an interpretive resource for the reader of Scripture, it is essentially a summative collation of other lexicons and grammars. The analysis of Hebrew and Aramaic adverbs, conjunctions, interjections, particles, prepositions, and pronouns contained in this book is based on works listed below.[1] Resources are grouped into Hebrew and Aramaic categories. Within those, entries are arranged alphabetically according to the italicized short reference.

Given that this *Lexicon* is based on other published works, the reader is encouraged to refer to them and make use of the page- and section-references provided to explore more deeply the syntactic function and semantic range of a particular word or collocation. The base texts for providing glosses and interpretive categories for the Hebrew and Aramaic words or collocations in this *Lexicon* are *HALOT* and *Holladay*, the latter being a condensed summary of the former with improved categorization in places.

Hebrew Resources

Arnold & Choi

Arnold, Bill T., and John H. Choi. *A Guide to Biblical Hebrew Syntax.* 2nd ed. Cambridge: Cambridge University Press, 2018.

---

1. The kind of pronouns included are correlative, demonstrative, indefinite, interrogative, and relative pronouns; the kind of pronouns not included are independent personal pronouns.

BDB

Brown, Francis, S. R. Driver, and Charles A. Briggs. *A Hebrew and English Lexicon of the Old Testament.* Oxford: Clarendon, 1907.

DCH

Clines, David J. A., ed. *Dictionary of Classical Hebrew.* 9 vols. Sheffield: Sheffield Phoenix Press, 1993–2014.

Gesenius

Gesenius, Friedrich Wilhelm. *Gesenius' Hebrew Grammar.* Edited by E. Kautzsch. Revised and translated by A. E. Cowley. 2nd English ed. Oxford: Clarendon Press, 1910.

HALOT

Koehler, Ludwig, Walter Baumgartner, and Johann Jakob Stamm. *Hebrew and Aramaic Lexicon of the Old Testament.* Translated and edited under the supervision of M. E. J. Richardson. 5 vols. Leiden: Brill, 1994–2000.

Hardy

Hardy, H. H., II. *The Development of Biblical Hebrew Prepositions.* Ancient Near East Monographs 28. Atlanta: SBL Press, 2022.

Holladay

Holladay, William L., ed. *A Concise Hebrew and Aramaic Lexicon of the Old Testament: Based upon the Lexical Work of Ludwig Koehler and Walter Baumgartner.* Leiden: Brill, 1988.

Joüon & Muraoka

Joüon, Paul. *A Grammar of Biblical Hebrew.* Subsidia Biblica 27. Translated and revised by T. Muraoka. 2nd ed. Rome: Gregorian and Biblical Press, 2011.

Van der Merwe
> Van der Merwe, Christo H. J., and Jacobus A. Naudé. *A Biblical Hebrew Reference Grammar.* 2nd ed. London: Bloomsbury T&T Clark, 2017.

Waltke & O'Connor
> Waltke, Bruce K., and M. O'Connor, eds. *An Introduction to Biblical Hebrew Syntax.* Winona Lake, IN: Eisenbrauns, 1990.

Williams
> Williams, Ronald J. *Williams' Hebrew Syntax.* 3rd ed. Revised and expanded by John C. Beckman. Toronto: University of Toronto Press, 2007.

Aramaic Resources

BDB
> Brown, Francis, S. R. Driver, and Charles A. Briggs. *A Hebrew and English Lexicon of the Old Testament.* Oxford: Clarendon, 1907.

Cook*
> Cook, John A. *Biblical Aramaic and Related Dialects: An Introduction.* Cambridge: Cambridge University Press, 2022.

HALOT
> Koehler, Ludwig, Walter Baumgartner, and Johann Jakob Stamm. *Hebrew and Aramaic Lexicon of the Old Testament.* Translated and edited under the supervision of M. E. J. Richardson. 5 vols. Leiden: Brill, 1994–2000.

Holladay
> Holladay, William L., ed. *A Concise Hebrew and Aramaic Lexicon of the Old Testament: Based upon the Lexical Work*

of Ludwig Koehler and Walter Baumgartner. Leiden: Brill, 1988.

Rosenthal

Rosenthal, Franz. *A Grammar of Biblical Aramaic.* Porta Linguarum Orientalium. 7th expanded ed. Wiesbaden: Harrassowitz, 2006.

*Vogt**

Vogt, Ernst, ed. *A Lexicon of Biblical Aramaic: Clarified from Ancient Documents.* Subsidia Biblica 42. Translated and revised by J. A. Fitzmyer. Rome: Gregorian and Biblical Press, 2011.

*In Cook and Vogt, some of the interpretive categories relate only to extra-biblical Aramaic texts. For the sake of comprehensiveness, in this *Lexicon* we include extra-biblical categories associated with Biblical Aramaic words. However, extra-biblical categories pertaining only to extra-biblical words are not included in the *Lexicon.*

INTRODUCTION

Translation, Interpretation, and (Re)translation

Purpose of this *Lexicon*

Accurate translation entails careful interpretation. The reading of any Old Testament text involves an initial gloss translation of each word, followed by a careful interpretation of the syntactic function and semantic range of the words in the text, as well as the relation of phrases, clauses, and sentences to one another, culminating in an accurate (re)translation. Take, for example, the Hebrew word אֲשֶׁר. The common glosses "who, which, that" do not always reflect the syntactic function of the word. For instance, אֲשֶׁר sometimes introduces direct speech and is therefore best left untranslated. The Aramaic word דִּי provides a similar example of a common word with various functions. In other words, an informed reader of the Old Testament must move beyond a gloss translation toward an accurate (re)translation by considering the syntactic function and semantic range of words in their respective phrases, clauses, or sentences. The purpose of this *Lexicon* is to aid such a translative-interpretive process.

The process of moving from gloss translation to accurate (re)translation through careful interpretation may be illustrated further with Hebrew אֲשֶׁר and Aramaic דִּי.

Function of Hebrew אֲשֶׁר

The Hebrew word אֲשֶׁר occurs approximately 5,500 times. As noted above, it is usually glossed as "who, which, that," with its most common function being a relative particle introducing a subordinate clause. However, this is not the only syntactic function of אֲשֶׁר; it may also be used as a conjunction in various ways (e.g., nominal, recitative, causal, consequence, comparative, purpose, conditional). Examples of the two main functional categories of relative particle and conjunction, along with their various subcategories, are listed below:[1]

A. Relative Particle

1. Marks the relative association between two clauses (an independent clause and a dependent clause); אֲשֶׁר is added to connect a noun to the preceding clause:

   וְהָיָה מִסְפַּר בְּנֵי־יִשְׂרָאֵל כְּחוֹל הַיָּם אֲשֶׁר לֹא־יִמַּד וְלֹא יִסָּפֵר

   Yet the number of the children of Israel shall be like the sand of the sea, **which** cannot be measured or numbered. (Hos 2:1a[E 1:10a])

2. Adds to the explicitness of the expression, the relation being more precisely expressed by a deferred preposition and suffix or the accusative sign:

   וַתַּהַר וַתֵּלֶד שָׂרָה לְאַבְרָהָם בֵּן לִזְקֻנָיו לַמּוֹעֵד אֲשֶׁר־דִּבֶּר אֹתוֹ אֱלֹהִים׃

   And Sarah conceived and bore Abraham a son in his old age at the time **of which** God had spoken to him. (Gen 21:2)

---

1. These examples are taken from *HALOT*, pp. 50–51; *Holladay*, p. 30.

3. Is followed by preposition and suffix, or another expla[n]atory word occurs directly after אֲשֶׁר:

שֶׁר־לוֹ הַיָּם וְהוּא עָשָׂהוּ וְיַבֶּשֶׁת יָדָיו יָצָרוּ:

The sea [**which**] is his, for he made it,
and his hands formed the dry land. (Ps 95:5)

4. Is present in a relative clause that lacks any reflex of [the] antecedent:

ע יְהוָה אֱלֹהִים גַּן־בְּעֵדֶן מִקֶּדֶם וַיָּשֶׂם שָׁם אֶת־הָאָדָם
יָצָר:

And the LORD God planted a garden in Eden, in the [east]
and there he put the man **whom** he had formed. (Gen[)

5. Introduces a gloss:

ה אֶת־הַשָּׂדֶה מֵאֵת חֲנַמְאֵל בֶּן־דֹּדִי אֲשֶׁר בַּעֲנָתוֹת
וְלָה־לּוֹ אֶת־הַכֶּסֶף שִׁבְעָה שְׁקָלִים וַעֲשָׂרָה הַכֶּסֶף:

"And I bought the field from Hanamel my cousin [**the one**] at Anathoth, and weighed out the money t[o him,]
seventeen shekels of silver." (Jer 32:9, editors' transl[ation)

6. May be preceded by a preposition:
   (a) בַּאֲשֶׁר **where, that which** (Gen 21:17)
   (b) כַּאֲשֶׁר **as** (Gen 21:1)
   (c) מֵאֲשֶׁר **from where, from what** (Exod 5:11), (
      that (Y) (Josh 16:30; 2 Sam 18:8)
   (d) עַל אֲשֶׁר **whither** (1 Kgs 18:12)
   (e) עִם אֲשֶׁר **with whom** (Gen 31:32)
   (f) תַּחַת אֲשֶׁר **whereas** (Deut 28:62)
   (g) אֶת(־)אֲשֶׁר **whom** (Exod 33:12)
   (h) לַאֲשֶׁר **to those who** (Isa 49:9)

7. Preceded by nouns in the construct state [locative/ temporal]:

וַיִּקַּח אֲדֹנֵי יוֹסֵף אֹתוֹ וַיִּתְּנֵהוּ אֶל־בֵּית הַסֹּהַר מְקוֹם
אֲשֶׁר־אֲסִירֵי הַמֶּלֶךְ אֲסוּרִים וַיְהִי־שָׁם בְּבֵית הַסֹּהַר:

And Joseph's master took him and put him into the prison, the place **where** the king's prisoners were confined, and he was there in prison. (Gen 39:20)

B. Conjunction

1. That (in object-clauses) [nominalizing]:

וְאַשְׁבִּיעֲךָ בַּיהוָה אֱלֹהֵי הַשָּׁמַיִם וֵאלֹהֵי הָאָרֶץ אֲשֶׁר לֹא־תִקַּח
אִשָּׁה לִבְנִי מִבְּנוֹת הַכְּנַעֲנִי אֲשֶׁר אָנֹכִי יוֹשֵׁב בְּקִרְבּוֹ:

"... that I may make you swear by the LORD, the God of heaven and God of the earth, **that** you will not take a wife for my son from the daughters of the Canaanites, among whom I dwell." (Gen 24:3)

2. "..."—quotation marks (introducing direct speech) [recitative]:

וַיֹּאמֶר שָׁאוּל אֶל־שְׁמוּאֵל אֲשֶׁר שָׁמַעְתִּי בְּקוֹל יְהוָה
וָאֵלֵךְ בַּדֶּרֶךְ אֲשֶׁר־שְׁלָחַנִי יְהוָה וָאָבִיא אֶת־אֲגַג מֶלֶךְ
עֲמָלֵק וְאֶת־עֲמָלֵק הֶחֱרַמְתִּי:

And Saul said to Samuel, "I have obeyed the voice of the LORD. I have gone on the mission on which the LORD sent me. I have brought Agag the king of Amalek, and I have devoted the Amalekites to destruction." (1 Sam 15:20)

3. because (causal):

וַתֹּאמֶר לֵאָה נָתַן אֱלֹהִים שְׂכָרִי אֲשֶׁר־נָתַתִּי שִׁפְחָתִי
לְאִישִׁי וַתִּקְרָא שְׁמוֹ יִשָּׂשכָר:

Leah said, "God has given me my wages **because** I gave my servant to my husband." So she called his name Issachar. (Gen 30:18)

4. so that (consequence):

הָבָה נֵרְדָה וְנָבְלָה שָׁם שְׂפָתָם אֲשֶׁר לֹא יִשְׁמְעוּ אִישׁ שְׂפַת רֵעֵהוּ:

"Come, let us go down and there confuse their language, **so that** they may not understand one another's speech." (Gen 11:7)

5. as (comparative):

אֶת־חַג הַמַּצּוֹת תִּשְׁמֹר שִׁבְעַת יָמִים תֹּאכַל מַצּוֹת אֲשֶׁר צִוִּיתִךָ לְמוֹעֵד חֹדֶשׁ הָאָבִיב כִּי בְּחֹדֶשׁ הָאָבִיב יָצָאתָ מִמִּצְרָיִם:

"You shall keep the Feast of Unleavened Bread. Seven days you shall eat unleavened bread, **as** I commanded you, at the time appointed in the month Abib, for in the month Abib you came out from Egypt." (Exod 34:18)

6. that [purpose]:

וַתֹּאמֶר לָהּ נָעֳמִי חֲמוֹתָהּ בִּתִּי הֲלֹא אֲבַקֶּשׁ־לָךְ מָנוֹחַ אֲשֶׁר יִיטַב־לָךְ:

Then Naomi her mother-in-law said to her, "My daughter, should I not seek rest for you, **that** it may be well with you?" (Ruth 3:1)

7. if (conditional):

אֶת־הַבְּרָכָה אֲשֶׁר תִּשְׁמְעוּ אֶל־מִצְוֹת יְהוָה אֱלֹהֵיכֶם אֲשֶׁר אָנֹכִי מְצַוֶּה אֶתְכֶם הַיּוֹם:

".. . the blessing, **if** you obey the commandments of the Lᴏʀᴅ your God, which I command you today, . . ." (Deut 11:27)

As the examples above demonstrate, translating Hebrew אֲשֶׁר with a simple gloss of "who, which, that" does not always provide an accurate interpretation (or translation). An informed reader must move beyond a gloss translation to careful interpretation to arrive at a more accurate (re)translation. The point may also be illustrated with the Aramaic word דִּי.

Function of Aramaic דִּי

The Aramaic word דִּי occurs approximately 330 times. It is usually glossed as "who, which, that," with a common function being a demonstrative particle expressing a genitive relationship. However, this is not the only syntactic function of דִּי; it may also be used as a relative particle or a conjunction in various ways, as illustrated in the books of Daniel and Ezra. Examples of the three main functional categories of demonstrative particle, relative particle, and conjunction, along with their various subcategories, are listed below:[2]

A. Demonstrative Particle (Expressing a Genitive Relationship) (Heb. זֶה, זוֹ)

1. After a determinate noun:

עָנֵה וְאָמַר לְאַרְיוֹךְ שַׁלִּיטָא דִּי־מַלְכָּא עַל־מָה דָתָא מְהַחְצְפָה
מִן־קֳדָם מַלְכָּא אֱדַיִן מִלְּתָא הוֹדַע אַרְיוֹךְ לְדָנִיֵּאל:

He answered and said to Arioch, the captain **of** the king, "Why is the decree of the king so urgent?" Then Arioch made the matter known to Daniel. (Dan 2:15, editors' translation)

---

2. These examples are taken from *HALOT*, pp. 50–51; *Holladay*, p. 30.

2. After an indeterminate noun:

נְהַר דִּי־נוּר נָגֵד וְנָפֵק מִן־קָדָמוֹהִי אֶלֶף אַלְפִים
יְשַׁמְּשׁוּנֵּהּ וְרִבּוֹ רִבְבָן קָדָמוֹהִי יְקוּמוּן דִּינָא יְתִב
וְסִפְרִין פְּתִיחוּ׃

A stream **of** fire issued
and came out from before him;
a thousand thousands served him,
and ten thousand times ten thousand stood
before him;
the court sat in judgment,
and the books were opened. (Dan 7:10)

3. If both nouns are determinate, often with a proleptic
suffix:

עָנֵה דָנִיֵּאל וְאָמַר לֶהֱוֵא שְׁמֵהּ דִּי־אֱלָהָא מְבָרַךְ
מִן־עָלְמָא וְעַד־עָלְמָא דִּי חָכְמְתָא וּגְבוּרְתָא דִּי־לֵהּ הִיא׃

Daniel answered and said:

"Blessed be his name, **that is**, God's [name], forever
and ever,
to whom belong wisdom and might." (Dan 2:20,
editors' translation)

4. To identify the material with which something is
made:

וּבְכָל־דִּי דָאֲרִין בְּנֵי־אֲנָשָׁא חֵיוַת בָּרָא וְעוֹף־שְׁמַיָּא יְהַב
בִּידָךְ וְהַשְׁלְטָךְ בְּכָלְּהוֹן אַנְתְּה־הוּא רֵאשָׁה דִּי דַהֲבָא׃

and into whose hand he has given, wherever they dwell, the
children of man, the beasts of the field, and the birds of the
heavens, making you rule over them all—you are the head
of gold. (Dan 2:38)

B. Relative Particle (Heb. שֶׁ, אֲשֶׁר)

To introduce a relative clause:

1. which, who (after a noun):

בֵּלְשַׁאצַּר אֲמַר בִּטְעֵם חַמְרָא לְהַיְתָיָה לְמָאנֵי דַהֲבָא
וְכַסְפָּא דִּי הַנְפֵּק נְבוּכַדְנֶצַּר אֲבוּהִי מִן־הֵיכְלָא דִּי
בִירוּשְׁלֶם וְיִשְׁתּוֹן בְּהוֹן מַלְכָּא וְרַבְרְבָנוֹהִי שֵׁגְלָתֵהּ
וּלְחֵנָתֵהּ:

Belshazzar, when he tasted the wine, commanded that the vessels of gold and of silver **that** Nebuchadnezzar his father had taken out of the temple in Jerusalem be brought, that the king and his lords, his wives, and his concubines might drink from them. (Dan 5:2)

2. who (as an explicitly expressed subject):

אַנְתָּה־הוּא מַלְכָּא דִּי רְבִית וּתְקֵפְתְּ וּרְבוּתָךְ רְבָת וּמְטָת
לִשְׁמַיָּא וְשָׁלְטָנָךְ לְסוֹף אַרְעָא:

". . . it is you, O king, **who** have grown and become strong. Your greatness has grown and reaches to heaven, and your dominion to the ends of the earth." (Dan 4:19[E 22])

3. that which, what (as an object):

עָנֵה מַלְכָּא וְאָמַר לְדָנִיֵּאל דִּי שְׁמֵהּ בֵּלְטְשַׁאצַּר הַאִיתָיךְ
כָּהֵל לְהוֹדָעֻתַנִי חֶלְמָא דִי־חֲזֵית וּפִשְׁרֵהּ:

The king declared to Daniel, whose name was Belteshazzar, "Are you able to make known to me the dream **that** I have seen and its interpretation?" (Dan 2:26)

4. who, that which (after an interrogative pronoun):

וּמַן־דִּי־לָא יִפֵּל וְיִסְגֻּד בַּהּ־שַׁעֲתָא יִתְרְמֵא לְגוֹא־אַתּוּן
נוּרָא יָקִדְתָּא:

"And whoever [**that**] does not fall down and worship shall immediately be cast into a burning fiery furnace." (Dan 3:6)

5. (other combinations):

עָנֵה דָנִיֵּאל וְאָמַר לֶהֱוֵא שְׁמֵהּ דִּי־אֱלָהָא מְבָרַךְ מִן־
עָלְמָא וְעַד־עָלְמָא דִּי חָכְמְתָא וּגְבוּרְתָא דִּי לֵהּ־הִיא:

Daniel answered and said:

"Blessed be the name of God forever and ever,
   to whom belong wisdom and might." (Dan 2:20)

C. Conjunction (Heb. אֲשֶׁר‎, כִּי)

The conjunctive use of דִּי‎ is not always distinguishable from the relative use:

1. that (after verb of knowing, hearing):

עָנֵה מַלְכָּא וְאָמַר מִן־יַצִּיב יָדַע אֲנָה דִּי עִדָּנָא אַנְתּוּן
זָבְנִין כָּל־קֳבֵל דִּי חֲזֵיתוֹן דִּי אַזְדָּא מִנִּי מִלְּתָא:

The king answered and said, "I know with certainty **that** you are trying to gain time, because you see that the word from me is firm—" (Dan 2:8)

2. (introducing direct speech) (like ὅτι) (Heb. כִּי):

אֱדַיִן אַרְיוֹךְ בְּהִתְבְּהָלָה הַנְעֵל לְדָנִיֵּאל קֳדָם מַלְכָּא וְכֵן
אֲמַר־לֵהּ דִּי־הַשְׁכַּחַת גְּבַר מִן־בְּנֵי גָלוּתָא דִּי יְהוּד דִּי
פִּשְׁרָא לְמַלְכָּא יְהוֹדַע:

Then Arioch brought in Daniel before the king in haste and said thus to him: "I have found among the exiles from Judah a man who will make known to the king the interpretation." (Dan 2:25)

3. so that, in order that (purpose):

וּמִנִּי שִׂים טְעֵם לְהַנְעָלָה קָדָמַי לְכֹל חַכִּימֵי בָבֶל דִּי־פְשַׁר
חֶלְמָא יְהוֹדְעֻנַּנִי׃

"So I made a decree that all the wise men of Babylon should
be brought before me, **that** they might make known to me
the interpretation of the dream." (Dan 4:3)

4. so that (result):

וְאַף שְׁמָהָתְהֹם שְׁאֵלְנָא לְהֹם לְהוֹדָעוּתָךְ דִּי נִכְתֻּב שֻׁם־
גֻּבְרַיָּא דִּי בְרָאשֵׁיהֹם׃

We also asked them their names, for your information, **that**
we might write down the names of their leaders. (Ezra 5:10)

5. for, because (causal):

דְּנָה חֶלְמָא חֲזֵית אֲנָה מַלְכָּא נְבוּכַדְנֶצַּר וְאַנְתְּה
בֵּלְטְשַׁאצַּר פִּשְׁרֵא אֱמַר כָּל־קֳבֵל דִּי כָּל־חַכִּימֵי מַלְכוּתִי
לָא־יָכְלִין פִּשְׁרָא לְהוֹדָעֻתַנִי וְאַנְתְּה כָּהֵל דִּי רוּחַ־אֱלָהִין
קַדִּישִׁין בָּךְ׃

"This dream I, King Nebuchadnezzar, saw. And you,
O Belteshazzar, tell me the interpretation, **because** all the
wise men of my kingdom are not able to make known to
me the interpretation, but you are able, **for** the spirit of the
holy gods is in you." (Dan 4:15)

6. (with prepositions) (Heb. **כִּי**):

אֱדַיִן מִן־דִּי פַּרְשֶׁגֶן נִשְׁתְּוָנָא דִּי אַרְתַּחְשַׁשְׂתְּא מַלְכָּא
קֱרִי קֳדָם־רְחוּם וְשִׁמְשַׁי סָפְרָא וּכְנָוָתְהֹון אֲזַלוּ בִבְהִילוּ
לִירוּשְׁלֶם עַל־יְהוּדָיֵא וּבַטִּלוּ הִמּוֹ בְּאֶדְרָע וְחָיִל׃

Then, [from] **when** the copy of King Artaxerxes' letter
was read before Rehum and Shimshai the scribe and their

associates, they went in haste to the Jews at Jerusalem and by force and power made them cease. (Ezra 4:23)

As the examples above demonstrate, translating Aramaic דִּי with a simple gloss of "who, which, that" does not always provide an accurate interpretation (or translation). An informed reader must move beyond a gloss translation to careful interpretation to arrive at an accurate (re)translation.

Organization of This *Lexicon*

Two main sections comprise this *Lexicon*: Interpretive Hebrew Lexicon and Interpretive Aramaic Lexicon. The layout for entries in each section follows an identical format. To illustrate we use the entry for the Hebrew word אַחַר.

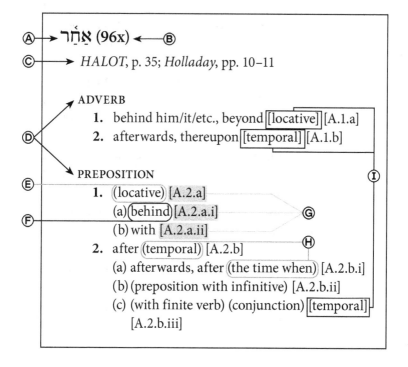

Arnold & Choi – spatial; temporal; metaphorical, pp. 110–11 (§4.1.1); temporal clause, pp. 190–91 (§5.2.4b, c)

BDB – *adverb*: of place; of time; *preposition*: of place; of time; *conjunction*: [temporal], pp. 29–30

DCH – *preposition*: time; place; personal relationship; [additional]; [in accordance with/according to, extrabiblical: Sirach 35:17]; *adverb*: time; space, pp. 1:193–95

Gesenius – *preposition*, p. 297 (§101a); *conjunction*: with אֲשֶׁר or כִּי, pp. 305–6 (§104b); temporal clause, p. 502 (§164d)

Hardy – locative; temporal/adverbializer; in accordance with/according to; conjunctive adverb, p. 38 (§3.1.2)

Joüon & Muraoka – preposition, pp. 309, 318 (§103a, n); conjunction, p. 319 (§104b); verbal clause, p. 550 (§155p); temporal clause, pp. 587–88 (166k)

Van der Merwe – spatial positioning; temporal positioning; causal, pp. 329–31 (§39.2)

Waltke & O'Connor – *preposition*: locational; metaphorical locational sense (manner/norm); temporal; interest: advantage or disadvantage; geographical, pp. 192–93 (§11.2.1); nominal infinitive construct with prepositions, pp. 604–5 (§36.2.2b); *conjunction*: temporal, pp. 643–44 (§38.7a); *adverb*: locative; temporal, pp. 657–59 (§39.3.1g, h)

Williams – locative; directional; temporal; adversative; norm, pp. 132–33 (§§357–362)

At the top of the page is the entry title Ⓐ, consisting of the word אַחַר written in its lexical form as it would appear in any standard Hebrew lexicon or grammar. The number in parentheses Ⓑ beside the word indicates the number of occurrences in the Hebrew (or Aramaic) Scriptures, as enumerated in Logos Bible software (note, however, that resources may differ in their counts due to varying identifications of roots or treatment of certain grammatical forms). Below this are two main sections. The first is the translational and functional entries from *HALOT* and/or *Holladay*. The second section provides references to other main lexicons or grammars that treat the functional entries. Hebrew entries draw from *Arnold & Choi* through *Williams* (in alphabetical order) and Aramaic entries draw from *BDB* through *Vogt* (in alphabetical order).

In the first section, the pagination in *HALOT* and *Holladay* Ⓒ indicates where the entry may be found in those works. The main grammatical-functional categories of the word in *HALOT* and/or *Holladay* are indicated by the terms in capital letters Ⓓ. In the example above, אַחַר functions generally as an ADVERB or as a PREPOSITION, following *HALOT* and/or *Holladay*. Where grammatical-functional subcategories are not supplied by *HALOT* and/or *Holladay*, such categories are introduced in parentheses Ⓔ based on the other works listed below in the second section. The numbered and lettered translational glosses Ⓕ for the subcategories follow those listed in *HALOT* and/or *Holladay*, along with their section references in *square* brackets Ⓖ. For example, the first translational gloss under ADVERB is "behind him/it/etc., beyond" and may be found at entry A.1.a on p. 35 of *HALOT* and pages 10–11 of *Holladay*.

If the grammatical-functional subcategory for the gloss is supplied by *HALOT* and/or *Holladay*, then it is placed in parentheses after the translational gloss Ⓗ. If the grammatical-functional subcategory is not supplied in *HALOT* and/or *Holladay*, then it is indicated by us in *square* brackets Ⓘ, either under influence from one of the other lexicons or grammars in the second section or by our own interpretation of the word's usage. When the grammars and/or lexicons employ functional explanations or glosses that can be combined under a common subcategory, we supply that subcategory in parentheses.

After the entry from *HALOT* and/or *Holladay* is complete in the first section, we list all the functional entries from the other main lexicons and grammars (with page numbers and section references) in the second section. If the main functional categories are supplied in the lexicon or grammar, then this is indicated by italics Ⓙ; if the grammatical-functional subcategories are not supplied, then we supply our own interpretation of the glossed translation or functional explanation in square brackets Ⓚ.

If a lexicon or grammar does not have an entry for a particular word or collocation, then it is not listed in this *Lexicon*. All in all, we have aimed for a comprehensive and condensed presentation as much as possible.

A further note on collocations is helpful at this point.[3] Hebrew collocations are included if *HALOT* and/or *Holladay* assign them their own entry; Hebrew collocations are not included if *HALOT* and/or *Holladay* do not assign them their own entry. For example, בַּאֲשֶׁר and כַּאֲשֶׁר have their own entries, whereas מֵאֲשֶׁר does not have its own entry.[4] However, some Hebrew collocations that do not have their own entry in *HALOT* and/or *Holladay* are included if they appear as a numbered section under another entry. For example, אַף כִּי appears as entry number 6 under אַף, and therefore is included as a collocation in this *Lexicon*; מֵאֲשֶׁר does not appear as a numbered section under another entry and so is not included.

---

3. A collocation is the combination of two or more words that commonly join to form a lexical connection.

4. To research מֵאֲשֶׁר, one would look up either אֲשֶׁר or מִן and find the word under one or both distinct entries.

With Aramaic collocations, a maximalist approach was taken, since the collocations are often formed from words occurring very rarely due to the small corpus of Aramaic within the Old Testament.

Conclusion

As stated in the preface, the aim of this *Lexicon* is to provide students, pastors, and scholars with a one-stop guide for the syntactic function and semantic range of all adverbs, conjunctions, interjections, particles, prepositions, and pronouns in the Hebrew and Aramaic Scriptures. To the extent that this book encourages readers of the Old Testament to move beyond a gloss translation toward an accurate (re)translation via a process of careful interpretation, it will have served its purpose. Given the technical nature of a project such as this and the meticulous care required, lacunae and errors are inevitable. We would therefore welcome feedback from attentive users of this *Lexicon* via zreview@zondervan.com.

DEFINITIONS OF
PARTS OF SPEECH

To understand how the words in this *Lexicon* function in a phrase or clause, the following definitions are provided for all parts of speech:[1]

- **Adjective:** a word that modifies a noun or pronoun
- **Adverb:** a word that modifies a verb, adjective, or another adverb; it communicates the concepts of time, place, quantity, manner, and intensity
- **Conjunction:** a word that joins words, phrases, or clauses; there are two types: coordinating (joining words, phrases, or clauses of equal weight) and subordinating (joining clauses of unequal rank, e.g., linking a dependent clause to a main clause)
- **Gerund:** a verbal noun (infinitive) or verbal adjective (participle) that functions like a noun in a clause
- **Infinitive:** a verbal noun: as part verb, it describes an action; as part noun, it can function in any syntactic role of a substantive in a clause, whether as subject, object, or adverb
- **Interjection:** a word that conveys emphasis or emotion
- **Noun:** a word that names a person, place, thing, including, for example, animals, activities, concepts, or qualities

---

1. Definitions are slightly modified from Gary A. Long, *Grammatical Concepts 101 for Biblical Hebrew*, 2nd ed. (Grand Rapids: Baker Academic, 2013).

- **Participle:** a word formed from a verb that functions adverbially or adjectivally
- **Particle:** a word with a grammatical function but not content (as do nouns and verbs)
- **Preposition:** a word that is placed before a noun or a pronoun to form a phrase; it nearly always functions as an adjective or adverb modifying another word in the clause
- **Pronoun:** a word that substitutes for a noun or a noun phrase
- **Verb:** a word that expresses a process of action or a state of being

While not all these kinds of words are included in this *Lexicon*, adverbs, conjunctions, interjections, particles, prepositions, and pronouns can relate to them in some way within a phrase, clause, or sentence.

DEFINITIONS OF GRAMMATICAL-FUNCTIONAL SUBCATEGORIES

For students beginning Biblical Hebrew definitions of terms used in the grammatical-functional subcategories are provided below. The list is not exhaustive. For example, self-explanatory terms, such as emphatic, locative, manner, spatial, temporal, etc., are not included, while less-known terms are. Users of this *Lexicon* are still encouraged to consult the grammars and lexicons listed in the bibliography to understand the nuanced definitions of these terms with respect to their use in Biblical Hebrew.[1]

- **Ablative:** a noun or pronoun that expresses instrumentality or deprivation
- **Adversative:** a clause that expresses an adverse or contradictory circumstance
- **Apodosis:** the main clause of a conditional sentence that contains a conditional clause
- **Apposition:** the juxtaposition of nouns functioning the same way in the clause
- **Asseverative:** a word or word collocation that conveys emphasis or strong affirmation

---

1. The definitions are taken or slightly modified from Todd J. Murphy, *Pocket Dictionary for the Study of Biblical Hebrew* (Downers Grove, IL: IVP Academic, 2003).

- **Asyndesis:** the coordination of phrases or clauses without coordinating particles or conjunctions
- *Casus pendens*: a grammatical element that is detached from and is grammatically unrelated to the main sentence
- **Comitative:** the joining of two or more grammatical elements by association, usually by employment of a preposition
- **Concessive:** a subordinate clause that appears to make the main clause unexpected
- **Concomitant:** the description of action occurring at the same time as another action and connected to it
- **Correlative:** a word or phrase related closely to another word or phrase within a sentence
- *Dativus commodi* (**or** *incommodi*): the dative of advantage or disadvantage
- **Deictic:** a word that defines spatiotemporal or social relationships
- **Desiderative:** expressing a wish or desire
- **Disjunctive:** a sentential element, usually a connecter, that relates clauses by contrast, separation, or the distinguishing of alternatives
- **Elliptic:** the dropping of a word or preposition when context allows
- **Enclitic:** a grammatical element attached to the end of or following a word
- **Exceptive:** a subordinate clause that makes an exception to the main clause usually introduced by "except" or "unless"
- **Existential:** a word or clause that indicates existence: "there is" (cf. "nonexistence" below)
- **Explicative:** a direct utterance which clarifies the meaning or identification of a prior utterance
- **Final clause:** also known as a purpose clause, a subordinate clause that expresses an action indicating the intended outcome of the action of the main clause

- **Instrumental:** a word indicating the object used to accomplish an action
- **Intensive:** a morphological or syntactical structure that increases the force of the action
- **Interrogative:** pertaining to a question or a word introducing a question
- **Limitative:** a word that qualifies another word, reducing its extent
- **Metaphorical:** the use of a figure of speech (figurative)
- **Nominalizing:** introduces a subordinate complement clause so that it functions like a noun within the main clause
- **Nonexistence:** a particle that means "there is not"
- **Optative:** a wish or strong desire often with the force of a command
- **Partitive:** a grammatical construction that identifies an item as a part of a whole
- **Periphrastic:** a group of words or a phrase used to convey and make more precise a single idea that may often be conveyed more simply
- **Pleonastic:** a grammatical element that is redundant or unnecessary
- **Preterite:** the past tense in grammar generally
- **Privative:** a verb or adverbial element which expresses the removal of something or a preposition which indicates deprivation
- **Proclitic:** a word joined to following word and having no accent of its own; in Biblical Hebrew proclisis is caused by the construct state or words joined by *maqqep*
- **Prohibitive:** a negative command
- **Protasis:** the subordinate conditional clause that relates to a main clause in a sentence, the "if" clause
- **Reciprocative:** describes mutuality between two actions or parties

- **Restrictive adverb:** indicates limitation on a verb
- **Sentential:** relates to a sentence
- **Separative:** conveys movement or positioning away from something
- **Specification:** describes or identifies a grammatical element more precisely
- **Substantive:** any part of speech used as a noun
- **Syndesis:** the coordination of phrases or clauses with coordinating particles or conjunctions
- **Terminative:** indicates an end/terminus of a preposition or verbal action
- **Volition:** pertaining to a wish

INTERPRETIVE HEBREW LEXICON

Analysis of Adverbs, Conjunctions,
Interjections, Particles,
Prepositions, and Pronouns

אֹבֵד (2x; Num 24:20, 24)

HALOT, p. 3; *Holladay*, p. 1

ADVERB
1. continuously, duration (traditionally, destruction)
   - עֲדֵי אֹבֵד forever

BDB – [*substantive*], p. 2
DCH – [*substantive*], p. 1:101

אֲבוֹי (1x; Prov 23:29)

HALOT, p. 4; *Holladay*, p. 1

INTERJECTION
1. woe

BDB – exclamation of pain, p. 5
DCH – interjection, p. 1:102
Waltke & O'Connor – woe cry, p. 682 (§40.2.4a)

אָבִי (3x; 1 Sam 24:12; 2 Kgs 5:13; Job 34:36)

see I אָבִי in *HALOT*, p. 4; *Holladay*, p. 1

INTERJECTION
1. would that! O that!

BDB – entreaty, p. 106
DCH – *interjection*, pp. 1:102–3
Gesenius – [interjection], pp. 497–98 (§159cc)
Joüon & Muraoka – optative clause, p. 579 (§163c)

אָבֵל (11x)

HALOT, p. 7; *Holladay*, p. 2

ADVERB
1. truly, alas [asseverative] [1]
2. but, however, on the contrary, no [adversative] [2]

Arnold & Choi – asseverative clause, p. 203 (§5.3.3d); adversative clause, pp. 194–95 (§5.2.10)
BDB – asseverative; adversative, p. 6
DCH – adversative; emphatic; interjection, pp. 1:109–10
Joüon & Muraoka – asseverative particle, pp. 580–82 (§164a, g)
Van der Merwe – speech turn; speech internal or narrative internal turn, p. 383 (§40.2)
Waltke & O'Connor – restrictive adverb, pp. 671–72 (§39.3.5e)
Williams – adversative clause, p. 196 (§554)

אֹדוֹת (8x)/אוֹדֹת (3x; Gen 21:11; Ex 18:8; 2 Sam 13:16)

HALOT, p. 13; *Holladay*, p. 4

PREPOSITION
1. עַל־אֹדוֹת on account of [causal] [1]

CONJUNCTION
1. עַל־כָּל־אֹדוֹת אֲשֶׁר for the very reason that, precisely because [causal] [2]

BDB – cause, always with עַל, p. 15
DCH – [specification]; [causal], pp. 1:148–49
Gesenius – causal clauses, p. 492 (§158b)

אֲהָה (15x)

HALOT, p. 18; *Holladay*, p. 5

INTERJECTION

   1. alas, ah! (cry in the face of fear/cry of alarm)

BDB – interjection, p. 13

DCH – interjection, p. 1:142

Gesenius – interjection, p. 307 (§105a); incomplete sentence, p. 470 (§147d)

Joüon & Muraoka – cry of sorrow, p. 321 (§105b)

Van der Merwe – interjection, p. 483 (§44.2)

Waltke & O'Connor – woe cries, pp. 682–83 (§40.2.4b)

אוֹ (320x)

HALOT, p. 20; *Holladay*, p. 6

CONJUNCTION

   1. or (particle of choice)

- אוֹ ... אוֹ either ... or (in a series)
- אוֹ כִי or if (introducing a clause)
- אוֹ ... אוֹ whether ... or (introducing two subordinate clauses)
- אוֹ ... הֲ whether ... or

Arnold & Choi – alternative, p. 154 (§4.3.1)

BDB – alternative; stating a particular case under a general principle; [possibility]; [exceptive], pp. 14–15

DCH – alternative; preference; [particle of choice]; disjunctive questions; stating a particular case under a general principle; [possibility]; [exceptive], pp. 1:147–48

Gesenius – *conjunction*: [alternative], p. 306 (§104c); interrogative sentence, pp. 473–76 (§150c, g, i); disjunctive sentence, p. 500 (§162a)

Joüon & Muraoka – coordinating conjunction, p. 319 (§104a); interrogative sentence: disjunctive question,

p. 575 (§161e, f); conditional clause, p. 594 (§167q); disjunctive clause, pp. 605–6 (§175a, d)

Van der Merwe – alternative, pp. 383–84 (§40.3)

Waltke & O'Connor – separating alternatives, pp. 654–55 (§39.2.6a, b)

Williams – alternative, p. 156 (§443); disjunctive question, p. 193 (§544)

אוֹי (24x)

HALOT, p. 21; *Holladay*, p. 6

INTERJECTION
1. ah!, alas!, woe (to you)!, (threatening) [1]
    • woe (is me) (anxious)
    • with עַל on account of, because of, with כִּי because
    • (preceding an interrogative sentence)
    • (followed by an explanatory clause)
2. woe (substantive) [2]

BDB – impassioned expression of grief and despair; denunciation; with a vocative; used as a substantive, p. 17

DCH – general expression of dismay; lamenting one's own situation; announcing disaster for others, p. 1:150

Gesenius – interjection, p. 307 (§105a); incomplete sentence, pp. 469–71 (§105d)

Joüon & Muraoka – interjection, pp. 321–22 (§105b); exclamatory clause, p. 587 (§162d)

Van der Merwe – experience of a threat, p. 483 (§44.3)

Waltke & O'Connor – woe cries, pp. 681–82 (§40.2.4)

אוֹיָה (1x; Ps 120:5)

HALOT, p. 21; *Holladay*, p. 6

INTERJECTION
1. woe!

BDB – impassioned expression of grief and despair, p. 17
DCH – *interjection*, p. 1:151
Gesenius – interjection, p. 307 (§105a)
Joüon & Muraoka – cry of intimidation, p. 322 (§105b)

אֱלַי/אוּלַי (45x)

see II אוּלַי in *HALOT*, p. 21; *Holladay*, p. 6

ADVERB
1. may be, perhaps (expression of hope, request/entreaty, fear)

BDB – expression of hope, fear, doubt, or mockery; followed by another clause it expresses virtually the protasis, [exceptive; rare: Num 22:33], p. 19
DCH – [uncertainty or possibility], in question or statement understood as question; [conditional]; [exceptive], p. 1:152
Van der Merwe – uncertainty or possibility, pp. 384–85 (§40.4)
Waltke & O'Connor – emphatic adverb, pp. 662–63 (§39.3.4b)

אוּלָם (19x)

see I אוּלָם in *HALOT*, pp. 21–22; *Holladay*, p. 6

CONJUNCTIVE ADVERB
1. but, on the other hand, however [adversative]

Arnold & Choi – adversative clause, pp. 194–95 (§5.2.10)
BDB – strong adversative, p. 19

DCH – [adversative], p. 1:152
Joüon & Muraoka – adversative clause, pp. 602–3 (§172b)
Van der Merwe – contravening assertion, pp. 385–86 (§40.5)
Waltke & O'Connor – restrictive adverb, pp. 671–73 (§39.3.5e)
Williams – adversative clause, p. 196 (§553)

אָז (144x)/אֲזַי (3x; Ps 124:3, 4, 5)

HALOT, pp. 26–27; *Holladay*, p. 8

ADVERB
  1. then (temporal past) [1]
  2. then (stylistic device for stressed/emphasized portion of sentence) [2]
  3. then [conditional future] [3]
      a. (following protasis) [3.a]
          • אִם . . . אָז if . . . then
          • (after infinitive construction)
          • לוּלֵי . . . כִּי אָז if not . . . then
          • לוּלֵי . . . אָז if not . . . then
          • לֵא . . . כִּי אָז if only . . . then
          • אַחֲלֵי . . . אָז if only . . . then
      b. (suppressed protasis, the condition to be restored) [3.b]
          • (the protasis is completely missing)
  4. with מִן (usually מֵאָז) [4]
      a. formerly, before, before now, earlier, long since (adverb) [temporal] [4.a]
      b. since (preposition) [temporal] [4.b]
      c. since (conjunction) [temporal] [4.c]

Arnold & Choi – temporal; logical; condition, pp. 139–40 (§4.2.1)
BDB – temporal; logical sequence, p. 23

DCH – temporal; logical, introducing apodosis after conditional clause, pp. 1:167–68

Gesenius – adverb, p. 296 (§100i); conditional sentence, p. 498 (§159dd, ee)

Joüon & Muraoka – demonstrative adverb, pp. 305–6 (§102h); verbal clause, p. 550 (§155p)

Van der Merwe – adverb of time; temporal adverb, pp. 386–88 (§40.6)

Waltke & O'Connor – past time with particles, pp. 513–14 (§31.6.3); temporal adverb, pp. 658, 667 (§§39.3.1h, 39.3.4f)

Williams – preterite in prose, p. 74 (§177c); apodosis of a conditional clause, p. 181 (§511)

אָח (3x; Ezek 6:11; 18:10; 21:20)

HALOT, p. 29; *Holladay*, p. 8

INTERJECTION
   1. alas! ah! (interjection of pain or grief)

BDB – interjection (onomatopoeia), p. 25
DCH – interjection, pp. 1:178–79
Gesenius – interjection, p. 307 (§105a)
Joüon & Muraoka – cry of sorrow, p. 321 (§105b)
Waltke & O'Connor – cry of pain or grief, p. 683 (§40.2.5b)

אָחוֹר (41x)

HALOT, p. 31; *Holladay*, p. 9

ADVERB
   1. back [substantive] [1]
   2. behind [substantive] [2]
   3. (adverb functioning metaphorically) [3]

- נְשׂוֹג אָחוֹר to give away
- שׁוּב לְאָחוֹר to turn back, to turn away
- הֵשִׁיב אָחוֹר to pull back, to repel
- הָיָה לְאָחוֹר and הָלַךְ אָחוֹר to turn one's back
  (alternatively, to decay morally)

4. west [directional] [4]
5. later (temporal) [5]

BDB – substantive; [adverb], p. 30
DCH – [substantive]; adverb: direction; indicating position;
  with prefixed preposition, p. 1:184
Joüon & Muraoka – [adverb], p. 304n2 (§102b)

אַחֲלֵי (1x; Ps 119:5)/אַחֲלֵי (1x; 2 Kgs 5:3)

HALOT, p. 34; Holladay, p. 10

INTERJECTION
  1. oh!, if only!, O that! [wish]

BDB – wish, p. 25
DCH – [wish], p. 191
Gesenius – interjection, p. 307 (§105a); desiderative sentence,
  p. 477 (§151e)
Joüon & Muraoka – wish, p. 324 (§105f); optative clause,
  p. 579 (§163c)
Van der Merwe – positive wish, p. 484 (§44.4)
Waltke & O'Connor – oath and wish exclamation, p. 680
  (§40.2.2d)
Williams – desire clause, p. 195 (§549)

אַחַר (96x)

HALOT, p. 35; Holladay, pp. 10–11

ADVERB
1. behind him/it/etc., beyond [locative] [A.1.a]
2. afterwards, thereupon [temporal] [A.1.b]

PREPOSITION
1. (locative) [A.2.a]
   a. behind [A.2.a.i]
   b. with [A.2.a.ii]
2. after (temporal) [A.2.b]
   a. afterwards, after (the time when) [A.2.b.i]
   b. (preposition with infinitive) [A.2.b.ii]
   c. (with finite verb) (conjunction) [temporal]
      [A.2.b.iii]

Arnold & Choi – spatial; temporal; metaphorical, pp. 110–11
   (§4.1.1); temporal clause, pp. 190–91 (§5.2.4b, c)
BDB – *adverb*: of place; of time; *preposition*: of place; of time;
   conjunction: [temporal], pp. 29–30
DCH – *preposition*: time; place; personal relationship; [addi-
   tional]; [in accordance with/according to, extrabiblical:
   Sir 35:17]; *adverb*: time; space, pp. 1:193–95
Gesenius – *preposition*, p. 297 (§101a); *conjunction*: with אֲשֶׁר
   or כִּי, pp. 305–6 (§104b); temporal clause, p. 502 (§164d)
Hardy – locative; temporal/adverbializer; in accordance
   with/according to; conjunctive adverb, p. 38 (§3.1.2)
Joüon & Muraoka – preposition, pp. 309, 318 (§103a, n);
   conjunction, p. 319 (§104b); verbal clause, p. 550 (§155p);
   temporal clause, pp. 587–88 (§166k)
Van der Merwe – spatial positioning; temporal positioning;
   causal, pp. 329–31 (§39.2)
Waltke & O'Connor – *preposition*: locational; metaphorical locational sense (manner/norm); temporal; interest:
   advantage or disadvantage; geographical, pp. 192–93
   (§11.2.1); nominal infinitive construct with prepositions,

pp. 604–5 (§36.2.2b); *conjunction*: temporal, pp. 643–44 (§38.7a); *adverb*: locative; temporal, pp. 657–59 (§39.3.1g, h)

Williams – locative; directional; temporal; adversative; norm, pp. 132–33 (§§357–362)

[אַחֲרֵי] (619x) [*sic*: אַחֲרֵי]

see אַחֹר in *HALOT*, pp. 35–36; *Holladay*, p. 11

PREPOSITION

1. back, rear end (substantive) [B.1]
- back (view)

2. behind [locative] [B.2]
  a. פָּנָה אַחֲרָיו turned around [B.2.a]
  b. דְּבַר מֵאַחֲרֶיךָ (from) behind you [B.2.b]
  c. to the west of [B.2.c]
  d. הָלַךְ אַחֲרֵי walk together with (image: one behind the other) [accompaniment] [B.2.d]
  e. bolt/lock the door [B.2.e]
    - הָיָה אַחֲרֵי attach oneself to someone
  f. סוּר מֵאַחֲרֵי leave off/desist from [B.2.f]
  g. with, at [B.2.g]
    - מֵאַחֲרֵי away from
3. after (temporal) [B.3]

CONJUNCTION

1. after [temporal] [B.4]
  a. (with infinitive) [B.4.a]
  b. (with finite verb) [B.4.b]
  c. (אַחֲרֵי כַאֲשֶׁר, אַחֲרֵי אֲשֶׁר) [B.4.c]

Arnold & Choi – spatial; temporal; metaphorical, pp. 110–11 (§4.1.1); temporal clause, pp. 190–91 (§5.2.4c)

BDB – *substantive*; *preposition*: of place; of time; *conjunction*: [temporal]; with other prepositions, p. 30

DCH – *preposition*: of time; of place; with verbs of motion; following or pursuing hostilely; accompaniment or direction or motion towards; below in status; in support of; [in accordance with/according to]; *conjunction*: introducing verb in causal clause; with מִן; [substantive], pp. 1:195–200

Gesenius – *conjunctions*: with אֲשֶׁר, p. 306 (§104b); relative clause, pp. 489–90 (§155n); temporal clause, p. 502 (§164d)

Hardy – locative; temporal/adverbializer; cause; particle, p. 54 (§3.2.2)

Joüon & Muraoka – *preposition*, p. 318 (§103n); *conjunction*, p. 319 (§104b); temporal clause, pp. 587–88 (§166k)

Van der Merwe – spatial positioning; temporal positioning; causal, pp. 329–31 (§39.2)

Waltke & O'Connor – *preposition*: locational; metaphorical; norm; temporal; interest; advantage; disadvantage; directional, pp. 192–93 (§11.2.1a); nominal infinitive construct with prepositions, pp. 604–5 (§36.2.2b); *conjunction*: temporal, pp. 643–44 (§38.7a)

Williams – locative; directional; temporal; adversative; norm, pp. 132–33 (§§357–362)

אֲחֹרַנִּית (7x)

HALOT, p. 37; *Holladay*, p. 11

ADVERB
1. backwards [manner]

BDB – *adverb*, p. 30
DCH – *adverb*, p. 1:201
Gesenius – [manner], p. 295 (§100g)
Joüon & Muraoka – manner, p. 304 (§102b)

אֵי (39x)

HALOT, pp. 37–38; *Holladay*, p. 11

INTERROGATIVE
1. where? where are you? [1]
2. (emphasized by/strengthened with demonstrative pronoun זֶה) [2]
    a. אֵי(־)זֶה where (then)? [2.a]
        • more specific: אֵי זֶה הַדֶּרֶךְ which way?
    b. אֵי(־)מִזֶּה from where? [2.b]
    c. אֵי לְזֹאת to what purpose, why? [2.c]
    d. אֵי זֶה, אֵי מִזֶּה (indirect questions) [2.d]

Arnold & Choi – interrogative sentence, p. 200 (§5.3.1c)

BDB – interrogative; strengthened by the enclitic זֶה; imparts interrogative force prefixed to adverbs or pronouns, p. 32

DCH – interrogative, pp. 1:202–3

Gesenius –interrogative pronoun, pp. 113, 444 (§§37a, 137a)

Joüon & Muraoka – interrogative adverb, p. 306 (§102i); the demonstrative pronoun, p. 499 (§143g); interrogative sentence, pp. 575–76 (§161g)

Van der Merwe – inquires as to the place where someone or something is; or the place from which or along which movement has occurred, p. 476 (§42.3.1)

Waltke & O'Connor – locative adverb, p. 318 (§18.1f); locative particle and related forms, pp. 327–28 (§18.4a–d)

Williams – question with an interrogative pronoun or adverb, pp. 193, 207 (§§545, 581)

אֵי I (1x; Job 22:30)

see III אֵי in *HALOT*, p. 38; *Holladay*, p. 12

ADVERB
 1. not [negative] [1]
 2. where? (in names of persons) [2]

BDB – [negative], p. 33
DCH – [negative], p. 1:204
Gesenius – negative sentence, p. 481 (§152q)
Joüon & Muraoka – negative adverb, p. 307n1 (§102j)

אִי II (2x; Eccl 4:10; 10:16)

see IV אִי in *HALOT*, p. 38; *Holladay*, p. 12

PARTICLE
 1. woe [exclamatory]

BDB – interjection, p. 33
DCH – interjection, p. 1:204
Gesenius – interjection, p. 307 (§105a)
Joüon & Muraoka – cry of intimidation, p. 322 (§105b)
Waltke & O'Connor – woe cry, p. 682 (§40.2.4b)

אַיֵּה (45x)

HALOT, p. 39; *Holladay*, p. 12

INTERROGATIVE
 1. where? (never before verbs, always in direct question)

BDB – interrogative, p. 32
DCH – interrogative, often with restrictive clause (relative
  or appositional) following, p. 1:208
Gesenius – interrogative sentence, pp. 475–76 (§150l)

Joüon & Muraoka – interrogative adverb, p. 306 (§102i); adverb with suffixes, pp. 307–8 (§102k)

Van der Merwe – inquires about the place in which someone or something is, p. 476 (§42.3.2)

Waltke & O'Connor – locative particle and related forms, p. 328 (§18.4c)

אֵיךְ (61x)

HALOT, p. 39; *Holladay*, p. 12

INTERROGATIVE
   1. how? (simple question) [1]
   2. (dependent question) [2]
   3. (doubting) [3]
   4. (reproachful) [4]
   5. (in mourning) [5]
   6. (asserting) [6]

Arnold & Choi – interrogative sentence, p. 200 (§5.3.1c)

BDB – interrogative; exclamation, p. 32

DCH – introducing rhetorical question; introducing simple question; interjection expressing enormity of catastrophe, typically within lament, pp. 1:208–9

Gesenius – exclamation, p. 471 (§148a, b)

Joüon & Muraoka – interrogative adverb, p. 306 (§102i); exclamatory clause, p. 578 (§162b)

Van der Merwe – inquires about the manner in which something occurred; rhetorical questions; exclamation to introduce the nature of a particular state of affairs or events, pp. 476–77 (§42.3.3)

Waltke & O'Connor – true questions of circumstance and in exclamatory questions, pp. 328–29 (§18.4d, e)

Williams – question with an interrogative pronoun or adverb, p. 193 (§545)

אֵיכָה (17x)

HALOT, pp. 39–40; *Holladay*, p. 12

INTERROGATIVE
1. how? in what way? [manner] [1]
    a. (indirect question) [1.a]
    b. = what? [1.b]
    c. (rhetorical) [1.c]
    d. (reproachful) [1.d]
    e. alas! how! (desperation/mourning, standard opening word of dirge) [1.e]
2. where? [locative] [2]

BDB – interrogative of manner; exclamatory; indirect statement, p. 32

DCH – interrogative, introducing rhetorical question, simple question; interjection, expressing enormity of catastrophe; [indirect statement], pp. 1:208–9

Gesenius – exclamation of lamentation, p. 471 (§148a, b)

Joüon & Muraoka – interrogative adverb, p. 306 (§102i); exclamatory clause, p. 578 (§162b)

Van der Merwe – inquires about the manner in which something occurred; rhetorical questions; exclamation to introduce the nature of a particular state of affairs or events, pp. 476–77 (§42.3.3)

Waltke & O'Connor – true questions of circumstance and in exclamatory questions, pp. 328–29 (§18.4d, e)

Williams – question with an interrogative pronoun or adverb, p. 193 (§545)

אֵיכֹה (1x; 2 Kgs 6:13)

HALOT, p. 40; *Holladay*, p. 12

INTERROGATIVE
1. where?

BDB – interrogative, p. 32
DCH – interrogative, p. 1:209
Waltke & O'Connor – locative particle and related forms,
   p. 328n28 (§18.4d)

אַֿיִן (אֵין) (788x)

see I אַֿיִן in *HALOT*, pp. 41–42; *Holladay*, p. 13

ABSOLUTE PARTICLE (אַֿיִן)
1. there is/are none, no, not (non-existence, absence)
   [A.1]
   a. וְאֵין and they were not there; אִם אֵין or is he
      not there?; אֵין לְ with infinitive, there is none to
      [A.1.a]
   b. אֵין there is nobody = no; וְאִם אֵין or else [A.1.b]
2. nothing (non-existence, absence) [A.2]
   • כְּאַֿיִן as/like nothing

CONSTRUCT PARTICLE (אֵין)
1. not, nothing, no (simple genitive relation) [B.1]
   a. no, not [B.1.a]
      • אֵין with לְ = not to have
   b. (dependent genitive precedes) [B.1.b]
   c. (לְ is lacking) [B.1.c]
   d. (genitive is lacking) [B.1.d]
   e. (constituents of the genitive construction are
      separated) [B.1.e]

2. [various constructions]
    a. (וְ)אַיִן preceding genitive = -less, without (circumstantial) [B.2.a]
    b. (with מִן) [B.2.b]
        • without [privative]
        • because [causal]
        • (with לְ)
3. not (develops into simple negation, לֹא and אַל) [B.3]
4. (אַיִן preceding infinitive) [B.4]
5. (אַיִן + לְ + infinitive) [B.5]

Arnold & Choi – particles of existence/nonexistence, pp. 166–67 (§4.4.1)

BDB – *substantive*; particle of negation; with substantive or pronoun; in circumstantial clauses; with infinitive and לְ; with prefixes, pp. 34–35

DCH – negative particle; may introduce various kinds of clauses: e.g., circumstantial, final, causal; negating indicative verb; with infinitive and לְ; [negative alternative]; as abstract noun: nothingness, pp. 1:213–20

Gesenius – negative sentence, pp. 478–83 (§152); circumstantial clause, p. 489 (§156b); conditional sentence, pp. 496–97 (§159v)

Joüon & Muraoka – negative adverb, pp. 306–7 (§102j); adverb of existence, p. 541 (§154k); negative clause, pp. 569–72 (§160g–k, o)

Van der Merwe – sentential negative; constituent negative; substantive indicating non-existence, p. 457 (§41.2)

Waltke & O'Connor – negative adverb, pp. 661–62 (§39.3.3b)

Williams – *substantive*; in the construct state; negative; to deny the existence of a substantive; elliptic; with an infinitive construct to deny a possibility or to deny permission; privative, pp. 146–48 (§§406–411)

אֵיפֹה (10x)

HALOT, p. 43; *Holladay*, p. 13

INTERROGATIVE
1. where? (direct question) [1]
2. (indirect question) [2]

Arnold & Choi – interrogative sentence, pp. 200–201 (§5.3.1d)
BDB – interrogative, p. 33
DCH – interrogative, p. 1:221
Joüon & Muraoka – interrogative adverb, p. 306 (§102i)
Van der Merwe – interrogative of content, p. 477 (§42.3.4)
Waltke & O'Connor – interrogatives and indefinites, p. 318
   (§18.1f); locative particle and related forms, pp. 327–28
   (§18.4a, c)

אַף (161x)

HALOT, p. 45; *Holladay*, p. 14

ADVERB
1. yea, surely, indeed (emphasizing) [1]
   • certainly (intensifying)
2. only (restrictive) [2]
   • just (limiting)
3. however, but, nevertheless (antithetic/contrastive) [3]

Arnold & Choi – restrictive; asseverative; adversative, p. 141
   (§4.2.2); exceptive clause, p. 193 (§5.2.7); restrictive clause,
   p. 94 (§5.2.8); asseverative clause, p. 203 (§5.3.3d)
BDB – asseverative; restrictive: contrast to what precedes,
   contrast generally; adverb of time, p. 36
DCH – asseverative; restrictive; adversative; restrictive in
   temporal sequence, pp. 1:238–39

Gesenius – restrictive and intensive clause, p. 483 (§153)

Joüon & Muraoka – asseverative clause, pp. 580–82 (§164a, g)

Van der Merwe – limitation; certainty; affirmation, pp. 388–90 (§40.8)

Waltke & O'Connor – restrictive adverb, pp. 669–71 (§39.3.5c, d)

Williams – restrictive; asseverative, pp. 140–41, 198 (§§388–389, 559)

אָכֵן I (18x)

HALOT, p. 47; *Holladay*, p. 15

ADVERB

1. surely, truly (exclamation to emphasize the unexpected) [1]
2. however, nonetheless (strongly contrastive) [2]

Arnold & Choi – asseverative clause, p. 203 (§5.3.3d)

BDB – strong asseverative; emphasizing a contrast, p. 38

DCH – emphatic; adversative, pp. 1:248–49

Gesenius – primitive adverb, p. 296 (§100i)

Joüon & Muraoka – asseverative clause, pp. 580–81 (§164a)

Van der Merwe – confirmation; affirmation; contrastive, p. 390 (§40.9)

Waltke & O'Connor – restrictive adverb, pp. 670–71 (§39.3.5d)

אָכֵן II (1x; 1 Kgs 11:2)

HALOT, p. 47; *Holladay*, p. 15

ADVERB

1. so that [result]

BDB – in 1 Kgs 11:2 אָכֵן stands unusually, p. 38.
DCH – emphatic, pp. 1:248–49
Van der Merwe – affirmation, p. 390 (§40.9)

אַל (726x)

see I אַל in *HALOT*, p. 48; *Holladay*, p. 15

NEGATIVE PARTICLE/ADVERB
1. (emphatic negation without verb) [1]
   a. no!, certainly not [1.a]
   b. (without expressed verb) [1.b]
   c. (וְאַל: verb supplied by previous imperative) [1.c]
      • (after infinitive absolute = imperative)
      • (after jussive)
2. not (with a verb) [2]
   a. (with imperfect as jussive) (prohibiting) [2.a]
   b. (request/pleading) [2.b]
   c. (with cohortative) [2.c]
   d. (with indicative) [2.d]
      • (emphatic statement) [2.d.i]
      • (negative wish and prohibition) [2.d.ii]
   e. in order that, so that (after imperative) (purpose or aim) [2.e]
3. nothing (substantive) [3]
4. certainly, surely (this use is questionable) [4]

Arnold & Choi – prohibition; negative volition, p. 142 (§4.2.3); negative sentences, p. 204 (§5.3.5a); elliptical clauses and sentences, p. 205 (§5.3.6d)
BDB – deprecation or prohibition; joined to a substantive (only Prov 12:28); poetically as a substantive, p. 39.

DCH – negative desire; prohibition; negative particle; substantive, pp. 1:249–53

Gesenius – negative sentence, pp. 479–80 (§152f, g, h)

Joüon & Muraoka – negative adverb, pp. 306–7 (§102j); direct volitive mood, pp. 348–49 (§114i–k); indirect volitive mood, pp. 356–57 (§116j); negative clause, pp. 567–71 (§160a, f, j); asseverative clause, pp. 581–82 (§164g)

Van der Merwe – sentential negative; constituent negative, pp. 458–59 (§41.3)

Waltke & O'Connor – jussive, p. 567 (§34.2.1b); uses of the imperative, p. 571 (§34.4); cohortative in independent clause, p. 573 (§34.5.1); negative adverb, pp. 660–61 (§39.3.3a)

Williams – negative wish; prohibition with jussive; elliptic; negative obligation; *substantive*, pp. 145–46 (§§401–405)

אֶל־/אֶל (5,516x)

HALOT, pp. 50–51; *Holladay*, p. 16

PREPOSITION

1. (with actions and events directed towards something, like to go, come, throw, bring, look, listen, go in (to a woman), have sexual relations) [terminative] [1]
    - to give to [datival]
    - to say, speak to [declarative]
    - to turn attention toward, seek, resort to, give praise to [perceptual]
2. toward [directional] [2]
3. (often represents עַל and vice versa, but may also be interpreted as motion toward) [estimative: interest/advantage or disinterest/disadvantage] [3]
4. up to, as far as [limitative] [4]

אֶל־/אֶל

5. in, into, inside, among [spatial] [5]
6. at, by (of rest at arrival) [6]
7. in addition to (with verbs of accumulation/adding and connection/uniting) [7]
8. in consideration of, with regard to, concerning, about [specification] [8]
   • because of, for [causal]
9. (combined with other prepositions) [9]
   • אֶל־אַחֲרֵי behind
   • אֶל־תַּחַת under
   • אֶל־מִבֵּית לְ inside
   • אֶל־מִחוּץ לְ outside
   • (in titles of Psalms)

Arnold & Choi – terminative; estimative; declarative; perceptual; addition; spatial; specification, pp. 112–15 (§4.1.2)

BDB – motion, where limit is entered into; direction; hostile motion; addition; metaphorical [specification]; rule or standard [in accordance with/according to]; presence at a spot; prefixed to other prepositions, it combines with them the idea of motion or direction to, pp. 39–41

DCH – movement, usually horizontal, where goal of movement is reached; vertical motion; of perceptual and verbal acts and dispositions of one person to(wards) another person, place, etc.; spatially above without contact; spatial vicinity without movement towards; [disinterest/disadvantage: hostile action]; [specification]; [causal]; aid or support; duty or charge over; [possession]; [interest/advantage: for the benefit of]; addition; comparison; in headings to psalms (to the tune); [limitative]; [instrumental]; followed by other particles; אֶל probably corrupt for אַל not (rare), pp. 1:260–71

Gesenius – motion; direction, pp. 378–79 (§119g)

Joüon & Muraoka – motion; direction; hostile direction; addition; metaphorical; norm; spatial, pp. 456–57 (§133b)

Van der Merwe – goal of movement or process; recipient of a transfer process; spatial positioning; joining together of entities; ground, pp. 331–33 (§39.3)

Waltke & O'Connor – direction; goal or termination; limit or degree; datival; comitative; specification, pp. 193–94 (§11.2.2)

Williams – spatially terminative; direction; indirect object; partisanship; advantage; disadvantage accompaniment; addition; specification; norm; locative, pp. 115–18 (§§297–308)

אִלּוּ (2x; Esth 7:4; Eccl 6:6)

HALOT, p. 52; *Holladay*, p. 16

CONJUNCTION
   1. if (contrary to fact) [conditional]

BDB – [conditional], p. 47
DCH – [conditional], p. 1:287
Gesenius – conditional, p. 494 (§159l)
Joüon & Muraoka – unreal conditional, p. 593n1 (§167k)

אַלְלַי (1x; Job 10:15)/אֲלָלַי (1x; Mic 7:1)

HALOT, p. 57; *Holladay*, p. 18

INTERJECTION
   1. woe, with לְ (onomatopoeic)

BDB – *interjection*, p. 47
DCH – *interjection*, p. 1:294

Joüon & Muraoka – cry of intimidation, p. 322 (§105b)
Waltke & O'Connor – woe cry, p. 682 (§40.2.4b)

אֶל־פְּנֵי (37x)

see פָּנֶה in *HALOT*, p. 941; *Holladay*, p. 294

PREPOSITION
1. before, to (at) the front of, by the side, along (with verb of motion) [spatial] [D.1.a]
2. on the surface of [D.1.b]

BDB – [spatial], p. 816
DCH – [spatial], p. 6:716

אִם (1,068x)

HALOT, pp. 60–61; *Holladay*, p. 19

CONJUNCTION
1. if (realizable condition) [1]
2. if (unrealizable condition) [2]
3. if only! (desiderative, with imperfect and suppressed apodosis) [3]
4. (oath formula as conditional [self-]imprecation) [4]
   • (with apodosis giving the effect of the imprecation/consequence of the oath)
   • (apodosis suppressed so that אִם = not, and אִם לֹא = certainly)
5. (questions) [5]
   a. (introducing a simple question) [5.a]
      • (pleonastic)
   b. are you . . . or . . . ?, do you . . . or do you . . . ? (disjunctive questions) [5.b]

6. whether (indirect question) [6]
  • who knows whether = perhaps (elliptical)
7. even though, even if (concessive) [7]
8. (collocations) [8]
  a. כִּי אִם except when, rather, unless [exceptive] [8.a]
  b. אִם לֹא if not, but, but rather (elliptical after
    negation) [adversative] [8.b]
9. (with imperfect) (prohibition) [9]

Arnold & Choi – conditional/contingency; concessive; alternative; exceptive; maledictory; oath; interrogatory, pp. 154–56
(§4.3.2); real conditional clause, p. 187 (§5.2.2a); exceptive
clause, p. 193 (§5.2.7); adversative clause, pp. 194–95 (§5.2.10);
concessive clause, pp. 196–97 (§5.2.12); interrogative sentence, p. 200 (§5.3.1b); oath sentences, pp. 201–2 (§5.3.2)
BDB – *hypothetical particle*: with imperfect; after an oath
becomes an emphatic negative, and אִם־לֹא an emphatic
affirmative; particle of wishing; nearly = when with the perfect [temporal]; *interrogative particle*: in direct questions;
in oblique interrogation; compounded with הֲ, pp. 49–50
DCH – conditional particle introducing protasis; sometimes
virtually equivalent to when [temporal]; in oaths following imprecatory formula; asseverative; interrogative; disjunctive; concessive; desiderative; relative; adversative or
exceptive; in combination with other words, pp. 1:301–7
Gesenius – sentences which express an oath or asseveration, pp. 471–75 (§149); interrogative sentence, p. 473
(§150c, f–i); desiderative sentence, p. 477 (§151e); negative sentence, pp. 480–82 (§152k, t); conditional sentence,
pp. 493–97 (§159)
Joüon & Muraoka – optative clause, p. 579 (§163c); asseverative clause, pp. 581–82 (§164g); clause of curse and
oath, p. 582 (§165a); conditional clause, pp. 590–95 (§167);
concessive clause, pp. 601–2 (§165a, d)

Van der Merwe – conditional, concessive; alternative/
coordinating; oaths, pp. 391–93 (§40.11)

Waltke & O'Connor – conditional clause, pp. 636–37
(§38.2d); exceptive clause, pp. 642–43 (38.6b);
restrictive adverb, pp. 670–73 (§39.3.5d); oath and wish
exclamation, pp. 678–80 (§40.2.2a–d)

Williams – conditional; concessive; alternative; oaths
and exclamations; pleonastic; optative, pp. 160–61
(§§453–458)

אִם לֹא (130x)

see לֹא in *HALOT*, p. 511; *Holladay*, p. 170

CONJUNCTION

1. אִם לֹא

    a. (whether) . . . or if not (continuation of a
       dependent question that started with הֲ) [11.a]

    b. surely (negative, with negative) [asseverative]
       [11.b]

    c. but [adversative] [11.c]

    d. unless [exceptive] [11.d]

Arnold & Choi – introduces a negative protasis of a
conditional statement, p. 154 (§4.3.2a); introduces a
positive oath, an action that one has committed oneself
to take, p. 156 (§4.3.2f)

BDB – [conditional-negative]; [alternative-negative], p. 519

DCH – oaths; [conditional-negative]; [alternative-negative],
pp. 4:486–95

Gesenius – introduces promises or threats confirmed
by an oath, and also simple asseverations, pp. 471–72
(§149); indirect question, p. 475 (§150i)

Joüon & Muraoka – disjunctive question, p. 570 (§160j);

direct question, p. 575 (§161d); clauses of curse and
oath, pp. 582–84 (§165)

Van der Merwe – marks a process that will occur (primarily
in a sworn oath), p. 392 (§40.11.2b); protases of incomplete
conditional clauses in a positive oath statement, p. 464
(§41.9.1c); contents of oaths, p. 489 (§45.3).

Waltke & O'Connor – protasis of a real conditional in
the negative, pp. 636–37 (§38.2d); oath and wish
exclamation, pp. 678–80 (§40.2.2)

Williams – introduces a positive declaration in oaths and
exclamations, p. 160 (§456)

אָמֵן (30x)

HALOT, p. 64; *Holladay*, p. 20

ADVERB
1. (originally an adjective) [1]
2. surely! [2]
   a. (solemn formula, by which the hearer accepts the
   validity of a curse or declaration) [2.a]
   b. (solemn formula, by which the hearer accepts an
   acceptable order or announcement) [2.b]
   c. (belonging to a doxology) [2.c]

BDB – *adverb*, p. 53
DCH – *adverb*; [*substantive*], pp. 1:317–18
Joüon & Muraoka – wish, p. 324n4 (§105f)
Waltke & O'Connor – nominal exclamation, pp. 680–81
(§40.2.3a)

אֹמֶן (1x; Isa 25:1)

HALOT, p. 64; *Holladay*, p. 20

ADVERB

1. trustworthiness, full of trustworthiness [substantive]
2. most faithfully

BDB – [*substantive*], p. 53
DCH – [*substantive*], p. 1:318

אֲמָנָה (2x; Gen 20:12; Josh 7:20)

see I אֲמָנָה in *HALOT*, p. 65; *Holladay*, p. 20

ADVERB

1. in truth, indeed [asseverative]

Arnold & Choi – asseverative clause, p. 203 (§5.3.3d)
BDB – [asseverative], p. 53
DCH – [asseverative], p. 1:318
Joüon & Muraoka – asseverative clause, pp. 580–81 (§164a)
Van der Merwe – speaker's confirmation of the truth, p. 393 (§40.12)
Waltke & O'Connor – emphatic adverb, pp. 662–63 (§39.3.4b)

אָמְנָם (9x)

HALOT, p. 65; *Holladay*, p. 20

ADVERB

1. surely, indeed, truly [asseverative]
   • כִּי אָמְנָה indeed, truly
   • אַף אָמְנָם if I had indeed, yea, surely

Arnold & Choi – asseverative clause, p. 203 (§5.3.3d)
BDB – asseverations, ironical, pp. 53–54
DCH – [asseverative], p. 1:319

Joüon & Muraoka – asseverative clause, pp. 580–81
(§164a)

Van der Merwe – speaker's confirmation of the truth,
pp. 393–94 (§40.13)

Waltke & O'Connor – emphatic adverbial disjunct,
pp. 662–63 (§39.3.4b)

אָמְנָם (5x)

HALOT, p. 65; *Holladay*, p. 20

ADVERB

1. really? (always with interrogative הֲ) [asseverative]

BDB – [asseverative] always in interrogative, p. 53

DCH – [asseverative], p. 1:319

Joüon & Muraoka – asseverative in questions, pp. 580–81
(§164a)

Van der Merwe – challenge the truth of a discourse active
proposition, pp. 393–94 (§40.13)

Waltke & O'Connor – emphatic adverbial disjunct in polar
questions, pp. 662–63 (§39.3.4b)

אָן (2x; 1 Sam 10:14; Job 8:2)/אָנָה (37x)/אָנָה (2x; Deut 1:28; Ps 139:7)

HALOT, pp. 69–70; *Holladay*, p. 22

INTERROGATIVE ADVERB

1. where? [locative] [1]
- where from? (מֵאַיִן)

2. (to) where?; (to) here and there [directional] [2]
- nowhere (with לֹא)

3. when? until when? how long? (temporal) [3]

- (interjection, or intermixing of two expressions) (only Job 18:2)

Arnold & Choi – interrogative sentence, p. 200 (§5.3.1c)
BDB – [interrogative of direction, location, or time], p. 33
DCH – [interrogative of direction, location, or time], p. 1:318
Gesenius – interrogative sentence, pp. 473–74 (§150c)
Joüon & Muraoka – interrogative adverb, p. 306 (§102i)
Van der Merwe – place to which someone is going; place in which an event occurred, duration of events, p. 478 (§42.3.5)
Waltke & O'Connor – interrogatives and indefinites, p. 318 (§18.1f); locative particle and related forms, pp. 327, 329 (§18.4a, f); polar questions, p. 684 (§40.3a)
Williams – question with an interrogative pronoun or adverb, p. 193 (§545)

אָנָה/אָנָּה (13x)

HALOT, pp. 69–70; *Holladay*, p. 22

INTERJECTION
1. oh, please, I pray (before imperative)
   - (preceding a request)
   - (as sigh preceding a statement, wish, or question)

BDB – strong entreaty, p. 58
DCH – expressing sorrow at past actions; with verb expressing action desired, p. 1:333
Gesenius – interjection, p. 307 (§105a)
Joüon & Muraoka – entreating interjection, pp. 322–23 (§105c)
Van der Merwe – urgent request, p. 484 (§44.5)
Waltke & O'Connor – exclamation, pp. 683–84 (§40.2.5c)

אַף (133x)

see I אַף in *HALOT*, p. 76; *Holladay*, p. 24

CONJUNCTIVE PARTICLE/ADVERB
1. also (addition) [1]
2. even, I for my part (emphasizing) [2]
3. even, certainly, moreover, really, how much more (enhancing/ascending importance) [3]
4. but (antithetic) [4]
5. (compounds) [5]
   - אַף־אָמְנָם really and truly
   - הַאַף־אָמְנָם shall I in fact?
   - הַאַף אֵין־זֹאת should this really not be?
   - אַף בַּל never yet
   - אַף־אֵין there is none at all
   - הַאַף will you really?
6. (אַף כִּי) frequently כִּי introduces a plain conditional clause [6]
   a. how much more if (conditional) [6.a]
      - (elliptically introduces a question, the contents of which are preceded by כִּי)
      - even when (stresses a clause of time)
   b. how much more when, how much more now (אַף כִּי has become a unit) [6.b]
      - how much less (after a negative clause)

Arnold & Choi – addition; asseverative; rhetorical, pp. 142–44 (§4.2.4); intensive clause, p. 194 (§5.2.9)
BDB – addition; especially of something greater, pp. 64–65
DCH – introducing second or third clause or noun; emphatic particle; specifying; consequence; [concessive]; [noteworthy addition: אַף כִּי], pp. 1:352–53
Gesenius – *conjunction*, p. 306 (§104c); restrictive and intensive clause, p. 483 (§153)

Joüon & Muraoka - coordinating conjunction, p. 319 (§104a);
asseverative clause, pp. 481–82 (§165g)

Van der Merwe - noteworthy addition; affirmation; addition,
p. 394 (§40.14)

Waltke & O'Connor - emphatic adverb, pp. 663–64
(§39.3.4c, d)

Williams - addition; emphatic; rhetorical; *a fortiori*,
pp. 139–40 (§§383–387)

אֵפוֹ/אֲפוֹא (15x: אֵפוֹ is rare, only in Job 17:15; 19:6, 23; 24:25)

HALOT, p. 78; *Holladay*, pp. 24–25

PARTICLE

> **1.** then, so (after interrogative particle מִי) [1]
> - (separated from the interrogative)
> **2.** what then? (before interrogative particle מָה) [2]
> **3.** would that now (after מִי יִתֵּן) [3]
> - if it is not so, then how? (after אִם and אִם לֹא)
> **4.** (exhorting) [4]
> - (separated from imperative)

BDB - in connection with interrogatory pronouns or
adverbs; in a command or wish; after אִם, p. 66

DCH - with interrogative; in commands, wishes; in
conditional sentences with אִם, p. 1:357

Gesenius - immediately after the interrogative to give
vividness to the question; may also be placed at the
end of the entire question or at the beginning of the
question proper, after a strongly emphasized word,
pp. 475–76 (§150l)

Joüon & Muraoka - logical particle, p. 306n4 (§102i)

אַף כִּי (26x)

see I אַף in *HALOT*, p. 76; *Holladay*, p. 24

CONJUNCTION

    1. frequently כִּי introduces a plain conditional clause [6]

        a. how much more if (conditional) [6.a]

          • (elliptically introduces a question, the contents of which are preceded by כִּי)

          • even when (stresses a clause of time)

        b. how much more when, how much more now (אַף כִּי has become a unit) [6.b]

          • how much less (after a negative clause)

Arnold & Choi – expresses a comparative assertion in which two clauses are related, the second bearing persuasive force; introduces a rhetorical question, in which the assertion of the clause is confirmed in light of the preceding clause; introduces an assertion modifying a single sentence without reference to a preceding clause, p. 143 (§4.2.4c)

BDB – [addition]; in a question; with reference to a preceding sentence, p. 65

DCH – [noteworthy addition], pp. 1:352–53

Gesenius – conjunction, p. 306 (§104a)

Van der Merwe – noteworthy addition, p. 395 (§40.14)

Waltke & O'Connor – emphatic, pp. 663–64 (§39.3.4d)

אֶפֶס (43x)

HALOT, p. 79; *Holladay*, p. 25

NEGATIVE PARTICLE

    1. extremity, end [substantive] [1]

    2. end, nothing, nothingness [substantive] [2]

        • בְּאֶפֶס without cause [privative]

3. only [restrictive] [3]
4. **אֶפֶס כִּי** notwithstanding, only that (limitative) [4]

Arnold & Choi – restrictive clause, p. 194 (§5.2.8)

BDB – [*substantive*]; non-existence; particle of negation; adverb of limitation, p. 67

DCH – [*substantive*], [non-existence]; negative particle; restrictive, p. 1:359

Gesenius – negative clause, pp. 478, 481 (§152a, s); adversative and exceptive clauses, p. 55 (§163c)

Joüon & Muraoka – negative adverb, pp. 306–7 (§102j); negative clause, p. 572 (§160n); exceptive clause, p. 603 (§173a)

Van der Merwe – extreme points of space; predicator of non-existence; restriction of invoked expectations, pp. 397–98, 460 (§§40.15; 41.4)

Waltke & O'Connor – restrictive adverb, pp. 671–73 (§39.3.5e)

Williams – *substantive*; privative; restrictive, p. 151 (§§425–427)

אֵצֶל (61x)

HALOT, p. 82; *Holladay*, p. 26

PREPOSITION
1. on/at the side of, beside [spatial]
   • over against (hostility)
   • **מֵאֵצֶל** from beside someone, beside

Arnold & Choi – spatial, p. 115 (§4.1.3)

BDB – proximity; with מִן, p. 69

DCH – [spatial]; with מִן; with אֶל, pp. 1:363–64

Gesenius – spatial, p. 297 (§101a)

Hardy – locative; proximal; directional, p. 67 (§3.3.2)

Van der Merwe – spatial, p. 333 (§39.4)

Waltke & O'Connor – locational, pp. 194–95 (§11.2.3)

אֲשֶׁר (5,499x)

HALOT, pp. 98–99; *Holladay*, p. 30

RELATIVE PARTICLE

1. (sporadically in old or poetic texts, originally the relative clause was joined to the noun w/o אֲשֶׁר) [A.1]
2. (אֲשֶׁר can be added to connect the noun to the clause) [A.2]
3. (אֲשֶׁר adds to the explicitness of the expression, the relation being more precisely expressed by deferred preposition & suffix or accusative sign) [A.3]
4. (preposition & suffix or other explanatory word occurs directly after אֲשֶׁר) [A.4]
5. (any explanatory word is omitted altogether) [A.5]
6. (historical development of relative clause) [A.6]
7. (introducing a gloss) [A.7]
8. (preposition may be prefixed) [A.8]
   - בַּאֲשֶׁר where, that which
   - כַּאֲשֶׁר as
   - מֵאֲשֶׁר from where, (X) than that (Y)
   - עַל אֲשֶׁר whither
   - עִם אֲשֶׁר with whom
   - תַּחַת אֲשֶׁר whereas
   - אֶת־אֲשֶׁר whom
   - לַאֲשֶׁר to those who
9. (preceded by nouns in the construct state) [locative/temporal] [A.9]

CONJUNCTION

1. that (in object-clauses) [nominalizing] [B.a]
2. ". . ."—quotation marks (introducing direct speech) [recitative] [B.b]
3. because (causal) [B.c]
4. so that (consequence) [B.d]

5. as (comparative) [B.e]
6. that [purpose] [B.f]
7. if (conditional) [B.g]

Arnold & Choi – relative particle, p. 172 (§4.6.1); substantival clause, pp. 185–86 (§5.2.1); real conditional clauses, p. 187 (§5.2.2a); final clause, pp. 187–89 (§5.2.3); temporal clause, pp. 190–91 (§5.2.4b, c); causal clause, pp. 191–92 (§5.2.5); relative clause, pp. 197–99 (§5.2.13)

BDB – *particle of relation*; *conjunction*: [nominalizing]; [consequence]; causal; conditional; [comparative: equivalent to כַּאֲשֶׁר]; combined with prepositions, pp. 81–84

DCH – *particle of relation*; *conjunction*: [nominalizing]; [purpose], causal, temporal, conditional, comparative, concessive, desiderative, [negative result], pp. 1:419–36

Gesenius – the relative pronoun, pp. 112, 444–47 (§§36, 138); *conjunction*, p. 306 (§104b); the noun – clause, pp. 454–55 (§141n); relative clause, pp. 485–89 (§155); circumstantial clause, p. 489 (§156b); object clause, pp. 491–92 (§157); causal clause, p. 492 (§158b); comparative clause, p. 499 (§161b); temporal clause, pp. 502–3 (§164d, f); final clause, p. 504 (§165b); consecutive clause, p. 505 (§166b)

Joüon & Muraoka – relative pronoun, pp. 108, 503–5 (§§38, 145); subordinating conjunction, p. 319 (§104a, b); demonstrative pronoun, p. 415 (§125g); relative clause, pp. 443, 557–64 (§§129q; 158); substantival clause, pp. 555–57 (§157a, c, e); final clause, p. 596 (§168f); consecutive clause, p. 598 (§169f); causal and explicative clause, p. 599 (§170e)

Van der Merwe – relative complementizer; independent relative; zero relative; resumptive; complement after verbs of observation; mental processes or speech; result; purpose; cause; motivation; real condition, pp. 304–6 (§36.3.1)

Waltke & O'Connor – introduces dependent or attributive relative clauses; temporal; locative; independent relative, pp. 333–35 (§19.3); conditional clause, p. 637 (§38.2.d); final and result clause, pp. 638–39 (§38.3b); causal clause, pp. 640–41 (§38.4a); temporal clause, pp. 643–44 (§38.7a); constituent noun clause, pp. 644–46 (§38.8a–d)

Williams – relative; independent relative; nominalizing; result; purpose; recitative; causal; conditional, pp. 163–66 (§§462–469)

אֵת (731x)

see II אֵת in *HALOT*, p. 101; *Holladay*, p. 31

PREPOSITION
1. together with [accompaniment] [1]
2. with the help of [assistance] [2]
   • with (instrumental)
3. by the side of, besides, at the side of, in the presence [spatial] [3]
4. (with מְאֵת, מֵאִתּוֹ, etc.) [4]
   a. out of, from (after verbs of removing) [separation]
      • through [instrumental]
      • bought from [acquisition]
      • due from [rights or dues]
      • by my orders [authority]

Arnold & Choi – accompaniment; possession; complement; spatial, pp. 115–16 (§4.1.4)

BDB – companionship; localities; denotes specially: in one's possession or keeping, knowledge or memory; with מִן, pp. 85–87

DCH – [accompaniment]; links verb (+ object noun) to additional noun; [under one's authority or responsibility]; [proximity]; [disadvantage: hostility]; instrumental; with מִן, p. 1:448

Van der Merwe – general shared proximity; shared activity; recipient; support; devotion; addition, pp. 334–36 (§39.5)

Waltke & O'Connor – comitative [accompaniment]; interest; complement of verbs of dealing, speaking, and making; addition; spatial, p. 195 (§11.2.4)

Williams – accompaniment; locative; possessor; advantage; disadvantage; coordination; reciprocal; assistance; partisanship; consciousness, pp. 127–29 (§§338–347)

אֶתְמוֹל (5x) [sic: אֶתְמוֹל/אֶתְמוֹל (2x; Isa 30:33; Mic 2:8)/אִתְּמוֹל (1x; 1 Sam 10:11)

HALOT, p. 103; *Holladay*, p. 31

ADVERB
1. yesterday

BDB – *substantive*; *adverbial accusative*; pp. 1070–71
DCH – [*substantive*]; *adverb*, pp. 1:461–62
Waltke & O'Connor – temporal adverb, p. 658 (§39.3.1h)

אֶת־פְּנֵי (11x)

see פָּנֶה in *HALOT*, p. 941; *Holladay*, p. 294

PREPOSITION
1. in the presence of, before, with the face of = before (with verbs of motion) [spatial] [D.2]

BDB – [spatial], p. 816
DCH – [spatial], p. 6:716
Van der Merwe – indicates that a trajector *x* is positioned in front of a landmark *y*. The landmark *y* is animate or inanimate and preceded by פְּנֵי, p. 334 (§39.5.1b)

בְּ (15,525x)

see I בְּ in *HALOT*, pp. 103–5; *Holladay*, p. 32

PREPOSITION

1. to abide, to stay at, in [locative] [1]
   - in the eyes of = in the opinion of [estimative]
   - before the ears, in the hearing of [auditory]
   - in the face of = before
   - in (locality reinforced)
2. to be in a multitude, (be) among (a group) [partitive/wholative בְּ] [2]
   - (to show a unique quality)
3. as (before singular expressing type or character, בְּ *essentiae*) [3]
4. (area) within (which) (realm something exists or happens) [4]
5. on, upon (with a high object) [locative] [5]
6. at, on, within (temporal) [6]
7. in (state or condition) [7]
   - in spite of (adversative)
8. according to [in accordance with/according to] [8]
9. into, among (after verbs of motion) [directional] [9]
10. (day) by (day) (from ideas of clinging and staying) [expressing entirety] [10]
11. (with verbs of seizing, catching, touching, attacking, persevering, placing one's trust in something) [11]
    - (expression of pleasure or disgust with verbs of perception)
12. (sharing of an act) [12]
    a. (together) with, in company with (accompaniment) [12.a]
       - בְּאֶפֶס, בִּבְלִי, בְּאֵין, בְּלֹא without
       - to speak with, to [declarative]
    b. against (hostility) [12.b]

13. away from [ablative/separative] [13]
14. more than (comparative) [14]
15. in, with, for (introduces particular circumstance) [15]
16. (introduces the means or instrument) [16]
    a. with (an ox); under (foot) [16.a]
    b. (God) through (prophets) [16.b]
    c. (swear) by (God) [16.c]
17. for (price or value) [17]
18. from (material) [18]
19. on account of, because (causal) [19]
20. (substitute for אֵת accusative) [20]
21. when (introduces temporal infinitive-clause) [21]
    • though (adversative)

Arnold & Choi – spatial; temporal; instrumental; adversative; specification; causal; accompaniment; essence (*beth essentiae*); manner; price, pp. 116–20 (§4.1.5); temporal clause, p. 190 (§5.2.4b)

BDB – *preposition*: position in a place; presence in the midst of a multitude; limits enclosing a space; with verbs of motion; time; material or mental state or condition; introduces the predicate; proximity; hostility; accompaniment; what one takes or brings; concomitant or surrounding conditions; instrument or means; cost or price; object of action treated as instrument by which it is effected; causal; material; [adversative]; measurement or computation; with verbs of trust, governance, emotion, perception and speaking; *conjunction*: temporal, causal, concessive, pp. 88–91

DCH – place/time; accompaniment; cause; instrument; agent; partitive; essence; comparison; [in accordance with/according to]; price; [adversative]; [specification]; [disadvantage: hostility]; [authority over]; [source]; [posterior time]; [accompaniment]; introducing object, pp. 2:82–86

Gesenius – domain; collective; sphere; manner; transitivity;

with verbs of perception; partitive; proximity; association; instrumental, pp. 380–81 (§119h–q)

Joüon & Muraoka – proximity; contact; adversative; participation; temporal; accompaniment; instrument or means; equivalence; transitivity; temporal; causal; with verbs of perception; intensity; durativity, pp. 457–58 (§133c)

Van der Merwe – localization; temporal frame; realization of an action; mode of an action, pp. 336–43 (§39.6)

Waltke & O'Connor – spatial; temporal; circumstance; specification; norm; estimative; identity; causal; distributive; partitive; object of a variety of verbs; perception and emotion; speaking, pp. 196–99 (§11.2.5)

Williams – locative; temporal-point; adversative; instrumental; transitivity; agent; price or exchange; cause; accompaniment; identity; specification; partitive; norm or manner; terminative; distributive, pp. 96–101 (§§239–254)

בַּאֲשֶׁר (19x)

HALOT, p. 107; *Holladay*, p. 33

CONJUNCTION
   1. because [causal] [1]
   2. (בְּ + relative particle) [2]

Arnold & Choi – causal, p. 119 (§4.1.5f)

BDB – [*relative particle*]; *adverb*; locative; *conjunction*: [causal], p. 84

DCH – [causal], p. 1:433

Gesenius – relative pronoun, p. 446 (§138f); causal, p. 492 (§158b)

Joüon & Muraoka – locative, p. 563 (§158m); causal, p. 601 (§170j)

Waltke & O'Connor – causal, pp. 640–41 (§38.4)

בִּבְלִי (5x)

see בְּלִי in *HALOT*, p. 133; *Holladay*, p. 40

ADVERB
   1. without (with substantive) [3]

BDB – [privative], p. 115
DCH – [privative], p. 2:177
Gesenius – cessation, p. 298 (§101c)

בָּדָד (11x)

HALOT, pp. 109–10; *Holladay*, p. 33

ADVERB
   1. solitude (substantive)
   2. solitary

BDB – [*substantive*]; *adverbial accusative*, pp. 94–95
DCH – [*substantive*]; *adverb*, p. 2:94

בְּטֶרֶם (38x)

see טֶרֶם in *HALOT*, pp. 379–80; *Holladay*, p. 125

PREPOSITION
   1. before (preposition) [temporal] [3.a]

CONJUNCTION
   1. before (with perfect, always passive) (conjunction) [temporal] [3.b]
      • with imperfect
      • with pleonastic לֹא

BDB – [temporal]; pleonastic, p. 382
DCH – [temporal], p. 3:375
Gesenius – *conjunction*: [temporal], pp. 305–6 (§104a)
Williams – temporal, p. 180 (§509)

בִּי (12x)

see בִּי אֲדֹנִי in *HALOT*, pp. 121–22; *Holladay*, p. 38

INTERJECTION

    1. by your leave, with your permission (formula for beginning a conversation with a person of higher rank)

BDB – particle of entreaty, craving permission to address a superior, p. 106
DCH – *interjection*, p. 2:142
Gesenius – interjection, p. 308 (§105b)
Joüon & Muraoka – intreating interjection, p. 323 (§105c)
Van der Merwe – expresses a request to be excused, p. 484 (§44.6)
Waltke & O'Connor – nominal exclamation, pp. 680–81 (§40.2.3a)

בֵּין (407x)

see בֵּין in *HALOT*, p. 123; *Holladay*, p. 38

PREPOSITION

    1. interval [substantive] [A]
    2. (preposition) [B]
        a. between (with verbs denoting distinction and similarity) [B.1.a]
        b. mostly בֵּין . . . וּבֵין; also בֵּין . . . לְבֵין, בֵּין . . . לְ, בֵּין between . . . and, whether . . . or [B.1.b]

c. (בֵּינוֹת, always between two parties) [B.1.c]

d. within (in semantic parallel with בְּתוֹךְ) [B.1.d]

3. (with other prepositions) [B.2]

a. אֶל־בֵּין up among [B.2.a]

• אֶל־בֵּינוֹת לְ in between

b. בְּבֵין [up among] [B.2.b]

c. עַל־בֵּין up among [B.2.c]

d. מִבֵּין from between [B.2.d]

Arnold & Choi – spatial interval; temporal interval, pp. 120–21 (§4.1.6)

BDB – spatial interval; idea of distinguishing in metaphorical applications, pp. 107–8

DCH – [spatial]; [conceptual]; [temporal interval], pp. 2:146–49

Gesenius – intermediate space, p. 297 (§101a)

Hardy – spatial interval; distinction; locative; separative; reciprocative; temporal, pp. 74–80 (3.4.3)

Joüon & Muraoka – distinction; interval, p. 318 (§103n)

Van der Merwe –Van der Merwe – spatial location; temporal location; conceptual distinction, pp. 343–44 (§39.7)

Waltke & O'Connor – inclusive: simple spatial-locative, manifold spatial-locative, temporal, distributive; exclusive: distinction, classes, pp. 199–201 (§11.2.6)

בַּל (73x)

see I בַּל in *HALOT*, p. 131; *Holladay*, p. 40

ADVERB

1. not (mostly in poetic texts, often repetitively) [poetic negative]

a. (with perfect) [a]

b. (with imperfect) [b]
- shall not, so that . . . not (modal)

c. (in nominal sentences) [c]

d. not yet, hardly, scarcely [d]

BDB – negation: poetic synonym of לֹא, p. 115

DCH – [negation], p. 2:174

Gesenius – negative clause, pp. 571–72 (§160m)

Joüon & Muraoka – negative sentence, pp. 478, 481–82 (§152a, t)

Van der Merwe – sentential negative in poetry, pp. 460–61 (§41.5)

Williams – objective denial of a fact; negate a predicate adjective; negate a prepositional phrase; negative wish; negate an infinitive construct, pp. 148–49 (§§412–416)

בְּלִי (58x)

HALOT, p. 133; *Holladay*, pp. 40–41

ADVERB

1. (substantive) [1]
   a. wearing out, decay [1.a]
   b. cessation, ending [1.b]

2. without, un-, -less (negation) [2]
   a. (with substantive) [2.a]
   b. (passive with participle or adjective) [2.b]

3. בִּבְלִי with substantive, without [3]

4. מִבְּלִי without [4]

5. לְבְלִי with substantive, without [5]

6. (negative with finite verb) [6]
   a. (with imperfect) [6.a]
   b. because . . . not (with perfect becomes conjunction) [6.b]

BDB – *substantive*; *adverb*: negation; with prepositions, pp. 115–16

DCH – [*substantive*]; *adverb*: [privative]; with prepositions, pp. 2:177–78

Joüon & Muraoka – negative sentence, pp. 478, 481–83 (§152a, t, u, y)

Van der Merwe – sentential negative, constituent negative, pp. 460–61 (§41.6)

Williams – objective denial of a fact, negate a passive participle, privative, p. 149 (§§417–420)

בִּלְתִּי (112x)

HALOT, p. 136; *Holladay*, pp. 41–42

NEGATIVE PARTICLE
1. no more existing (substantive) [1]
2. not (with adjective) [negation] [2]
3. except, besides (excluding) [3]
   a. הַיּוֹם בִּלְתִּי except for today; unless (with nom. clause) [3.a]
   b. בִּלְתִּי אִם unless, except [3.b]
   c. with כָּרַע unless [develops into] only (this usage is questionable; only Isa 10:4) [3.c]
4. without [privative] [4]
5. לְבִלְתִּי (with infinitive) [5]
   a. that . . . not [5.a]
   b. that . . . not (following נִשְׁבַּע) [5.b]
   c. lest [5.c]
6. that . . . not, lest (with imperfect) [negative result] [6]
7. lest (לְבִלְתִּי לֹ with infinitive) [negative result] [7]
8. until, so that not (עַד־בִּלְתִּי with perfect) [temporal or negative result] [8]

Arnold & Choi – negative final/result clause, pp. 188–89
(§5.2.3c); exceptive clause, p. 193 (5.2.7); negative
sentence, p. 204 (§5.3.6c)

BDB – *adverb*: negation; [exceptive]; *conjunction*: [exceptive];
with prepositions, p. 116

DCH – [negation]; negative existential quantifier;
introducing object or final clause; with prepositions,
pp. 2:183–84

Gesenius – negative sentence, pp. 478, 481–83 (§152a, t);
adversative and exceptive clauses, p. 500 (§163c)

Joüon & Muraoka – negative clause, pp. 571–72 (§160m)

Van der Merwe – sentential negative; constituent negative,
pp. 460–61 (§41.7)

Williams – privative; exceptive; to negate an infinitive
construct; to negate a purpose or result, pp. 149–50
(§§421–424)

בַּמֶּה/בַּמָּה (29x)

see מָה in *HALOT*, p. 551; *Holladay*, p. 184

PREPOSITION

1. with what?, by what means?, wherein?, wherefore?,
   why?, how? [interrogative] [D.1]

BDB – interrogative; and so according to the various
senses of בְּ, p. 553

DCH – [interrogative; and so according to the various
senses of בְּ], p. 5:160

Gesenius – interrogative, p. 113 (§37e)

Joüon & Muraoka – interrogative, p. 107 (§37d)

Van der Merwe – interrogative of manner, p. 395 (§42.3.7.2)

Waltke & O'Connor – interrogative, p. 325 (§18.3d)

בַּעֲבוּר (49x)

see עֲבוּר in *HALOT*, pp. 777–78; *Holladay*, p. 262

PREPOSITION
1. because of, for the sake of [casual] [B.1.a]
2. because of, on account of (with genitive) [causal] [B.1.b]
3. for (the price of) (price) [B.1.c]

CONJUNCTION
1. so that, (in order) that [purpose] [B.2]
   a. (with imperfect) [B.2.a]
   b. בַּעֲבוּר אֲשֶׁר so that [B.2.b]
   c. so that (with infinitive) [B.2.c]
   d. לְבַעֲבוּר (with infinitive) [B.2.d]

Arnold & Choi – final clause, pp. 187–88 (§5.2.3a)

BDB – *preposition*: [causal]; [purpose]; *conjunction*: [purpose], p. 721

DCH – *preposition*: [causal]; [price]; *conjunction*: [purpose], p. 2:234

Gesenius – final clause, p. 504 (§165b)

Hardy – *substantive*; cause, exchange; purpose, pp. 134–36 (§4.6.2)

Joüon & Muraoka – final clause, p. 596 (§165b); causal and explicative clause, p. 601 (§170.l)

Van der Merwe – purpose; reason, pp. 399–400 (§40.19)

Waltke & O'Connor – final and result clauses, pp. 638–39 (§38.3b)

Williams – purpose clause, pp. 185–86 (§522a, b)

בְּעַד (106x)

see I בְּעַד in *HALOT*, p. 141; *Holladay*, p. 43

PREPOSITION

>1. at a distance from [develops into] behind; with verbs
>   of shutting [spatial] [1]
>2. through, out of (especially a window), (motion) over
>   (a wall) [spatial] [2]
>3. around [spatial] [3]
>4. for (the benefit of) [advantage] [4]
>5. for (price) [exchange] [5]

Arnold & Choi – spatial; advantage, pp. 121–22 (§4.1.7)
BDB – separation; metaphoric [advantage], p. 126
DCH – [spatial]; [advantage]; [causal]; [exchange],
   pp. 2:235–36
Gesenius – distance, p. 297 (§101a)
Hardy – spatiodirectional path; locative; intended recipient,
   pp. 87–90 (§3.5.2)
Joüon & Muraoka – distance, p. 313 (§103e)
Van der Merwe – spatial location of a path; involvement of
   x to the benefit of *y*, pp. 344–45 (§39.9)
Waltke & O'Connor – locational; interest or advantage,
   pp. 201–2 (§11.2.7)
Williams – locative; advantage, pp. 131–32 (§§354–356)

בִּפְנֵי (17x)

see פָּנֶה in *HALOT*, p. 941; *Holladay*, p. 294

PREPOSITION

>1. in the face of, before, against [spatial] [D.3]
>   • to withstand someone [hostile]

BDB – [spatial, sometimes with hostile import], p. 816
DCH – [spatial, sometimes with hostile import], p. 6:716

בָּרוּר (2x; Zeph 3:9; Job 33:3)

HALOT, p. 155; *Holladay*, p. 47

ADVERB
1. pure, plan [adjective] [1]
2. candidly, purely [manner] [2]

BDB – passive participle, pp. 140–41
DCH – passive participle as adjective or adverb, p. 2:275

גַּם (769x)

HALOT, pp. 195–96; *Holladay*, pp. 61–62

ADVERB
1. as well as, both (associative) [1]
2. also (adding) [2]
3. also (emphasizing) [3]
4. on his part (emphasis prevails association) [4]
5. even (intensified) [5]
6. (in (actual or implied) repetition as a figure of speech) [6]
7. (with negation) [7]
   • גַּם ... לֹא not ... either
   • גַּם ... אֵין there is not even
   • לֹא ... גַּם אֶחָד not even one
   • גַּם עַד־הָעֵת הַהִיא לֹא it is true that up to that time ... not
8. (and) also = even (emphatically combining clauses) [8]
9. (in collocations) [9]
   • כִּי גַם even though
   • גַּם אֲשֶׁר even what
   • גַּם כִּי even when
   • גַּם עַתָּה even now

- גַּם עַתָּה so now (formula for continuation)
10. (often occurs at beginning of clause and not where it belongs logically) [10]
11. (וְגַם is used in the same way as גַּם) [11]
   a. and also, and further (supplementation) [11.a]
   b. וְגַם עַתָּה and yet even now (emphasizing) [11.b]
      - וְגַם אַתֶּם you however; וְגַם אֲנִי I on my part (emphasizing exclusively)
12. (when וְגַם connects two clauses the emphasized part of the clause is put at the beginning) [12]
13. גַּם . . . גַּם both . . . and [multiple inclusion] [13]
      - גַּם הֵמָּה גַּם אֲנִי whereas they . . . so also I (stresses the contrast)
      - גַּם . . . גַּם . . . לֹא neither . . . nor [multiple exclusion]

Arnold & Choi – addition; asseverative; concessive, pp. 144–45 (§4.2.5); intensive clause, p. 194 (§5.2.9); concessive clause, pp. 196–97 (§5.2.12)

BDB – addition; emphasis; word-stress; introducing a climax; correspondence; [adversative]; with כִּי, pp. 168–69

DCH – [addition]; [concessive]; [logical consequence]; with prepositions, pp. 2:357–61

Gesenius – restrictive and intensive clauses, p. 483 (§153); concessive clause, p. 498 (§160); disjunctive sentence, p. 500 (§162)

Joüon & Muraoka – asseverative clause, pp. 581–82 (§164g); concessive clause, pp. 601–2 (§171a, c); syndesis and asyndesis, pp. 613–14 (§177q)

Van der Merwe – addition; corresponding reaction; multiple inclusion; affirmation; 'apparent' neutral enumeration, pp. 401–5 (§40.20)

Waltke & O'Connor – emphatic adverb, p. 663 (§39.3.4c, d)

Williams – emphatic; rhetorical; correlative; concessive, pp. 138–39 (§§378–382)

הֵא (2x; Gen 47:23; Ezek 16:43)

HALOT, p. 236; *Holladay*, p. 76

INTERJECTION
  1. lo! behold! there! see!

BDB – interjection, p. 210
DCH – interjection, p. 2:484
Gesenius – interjection, p. 307 (§105b)
Waltke & O'Connor – exclamation (sense is unknown:
    context different in both occurrences), p. 684
    (§40.2.5d)

הֶאָח (12x)

HALOT, p. 236; *Holladay*, p. 76

INTERJECTION
  1. aha! (expression of joy)
  2. aha! (of malicious joy)
  3. aha! (cry of the war-horse)

BDB – expressing joy; of satisfaction over the misfortune of
    an enemy or rival; the neighing of a war hose in the battle,
    p. 210
DCH – expression of satisfaction or joy, usually in response
    to another's misfortune, pp. 2:484–85
Gesenius – interjection, p. 307 (§105a)
Joüon & Muraoka – cry of joy, p. 321 (§105b)
Waltke & O'Connor – associated with a horse going into
    battle; apparently a human cry of joy (sometimes mean
    spirited), p. 683 (§40.2.5b)

הָבָה (5x)

see I הַב in *HALOT*, p. 236; *Holladay*, p. 76

INTERJECTION
1. come! come on! [2]

BDB – emphatic, p. 396
DCH – *interjection*, p. 4:115
Gesenius – interjection, p. 307 (§105b)
Joüon & Muraoka – interjection, p. 324 (§105e)

הָה (1x; Ezek 30:2)

HALOT, p. 240; *Holladay*, p. 77

INTERJECTION
1. alas!

BDB – expressing woe, p. 214
DCH – *interjection*, p. 2:493
Gesenius – interjection, p. 307 (§105a)
Joüon & Muraoka – cry of sorrow, p. 321 (§105b)

הוֹ (2x; both in Amos 5:16)

HALOT, p. 240; *Holladay*, p. 77

INTERJECTION
1. הוֹ־הוֹ alas! (intensified by reduplication)

BDB – *interjection*, p. 214
DCH – *interjection*, p. 2:493
Gesenius – interjection, p. 307 (§105a)

הוֹי (51x)

HALOT, p. 242; *Holladay*, pp. 77–78

INTERJECTION
1. ah! alas! woe! (in lament) [1]
2. (grievous threatening cry/prophetic threat) [2]
   a. (with participle or adjective) [2.a]
   b. (with vocative) [2.b]
   c. (with עַל; with לְ) [2.c]
   d. (absolute usage) [2.d]
3. ha!, ho! (encouraging/inciting) [3]

BDB – dissatisfaction and pain; preparatory to a declaration of judgment; exclamation arousing attention, pp. 222–23

DCH – expression of dismay; victim of disaster named immediately after הוֹי, pp. 2:503–4

Gesenius – interjection, p. 307 (§105a); incomplete sentence, pp. 470–71 (§147d)

Joüon & Muraoka – interjection, p. 322 (§105.b); exclamatory clause, p. 578 (§162d)

Van der Merwe – expresses the experience of threat, p. 484 (§44.7)

Waltke & O'Connor – woe cries, pp. 681–82 (§40.2.4a)

הִי (1x; Ezek 2:10)

HALOT, p. 243; *Holladay*, p. 78

INTERJECTION
1. woe!

BDB – [*substantive*], p. 223
DCH – [*substantive*], p. 2:508

הָלְאָה (16x)

HALOT, p. 245; *Holladay*, p. 79

ADVERB

1. (to) there, thither, further (place) [1]
   a. זְרֵה־הָלְאָה scatter yonder, גֶּשׁ־הָלְאָה go away! [1.a]
   b. מֵהָלְאָה לְ beyond [1.b]
   c. וָהָלְאָה and forward [1.c]
   d. מִשָּׁם וָהָלְאָה and from there further, מִן־הוּא וָהָלְאָה far and wide [1.d]
2. onward, from then on (time) [2]

BDB – place; time, p. 229
DCH – place; time, p. 2:544
Joüon & Muraoka – demonstrative adverb, p. 306 (§102h)

הֲלֹם (12x)

HALOT, p. 249; *Holladay*, p. 81

ADVERB

1. hither, to here (place) [1]
   • עַד־הֲלֹם as far as this
2. here (place) [2]

BDB – adverb of place; figurative, pp. 240–41
DCH – adverb [of place], p. 2:563
Joüon & Muraoka – demonstrative adverb [of place],
   pp. 305–6 (§102h)
Waltke & O'Connor – adverb of location, pp. 657–58 (§39.3.1g)

הֵן (100x)

see I הֵן in *HALOT*, p. 251; *Holladay*, p. 82

DEMONSTRATIVE INTERJECTION & CONJUNCTION
1. behold (emphasizing following word, phrase, clause) [1]
   • good! all right! (consent/agreeing)
2. if (conditional) [2]

Arnold & Choi – real conditional clauses, p. 187 (§5.2.2a)

BDB – *demonstrative adverb or interjection*: calling attention to some fact upon which action is to be taken, or a conclusion based; *hypothetical particle*: propounding a possibility; in an indirect question, p. 243

DCH – followed by question functioning as apodosis of conditional sentence, pp. 2:572–73

Gesenius – incomplete sentence, pp. 469–70 (§147b); conditional sentence, pp. 494–95, 497 (§159l, w)

Joüon & Muraoka – interjection, pp. 323–24 (§105d); asseverative clause, pp. 581–82 (§164a, g); conditional clause, pp. 593–94 (§167.l)

Van der Merwe – affirmation; grounds; presentative, pp. 405–7 (§40.21)

Waltke & O'Connor – textual organization, p. 634 (§38.1e); conditional clause, p. 637 (38.2d); presentative exclamation, p. 675 (§40.2.1a)

Williams – real condition, p. 182 (§514)

הֵנָּה (50x)

see I הֵנָּה in *HALOT*, pp. 251–52; *Holladay*, p. 82

ADVERB
1. here (place) [1]
2. hither, (to) here (place) [2]
3. עַד־הֵנָּה as far as (to) here, over here, thus far (place) [3]
4. הֵנָּה ... הֵנָּה here ... there = on this side ... on that side (place) [4]

- with אַחַת (to go) up and down, back and forth
- הֵנָּה וָהֵנָּה hither and thither, to one side and to the other
- מִמְּךָ וָהֵנָּה on this side of you

5. until now (time) [5]

BDB – place; time, p. 244
DCH – place; time, p. 2:574
Gesenius – place; time, p. 295 (§100f)
Joüon & Muraoka – [place], p. 306 (§102h)
Waltke & O'Connor – adverb of location; temporal adverb, p. 658 (§39.3.1g, h)

וְהִנֵּה/הִנֵּה (1060x)

HALOT, p. 252; *Holladay*, p. 82

DEMONSTRATIVE INTERJECTION
1. behold, see (calls attention to following noun) [1]
2. הִנְנִי here I am! (someone who has been summoned announces his presence/answer of a person called) [2]
3. (follows a noun to emphasize it) [3]
4. (following a pronoun הִנֵּה stresses) [4]
   a. (the subject of the following verb) [4.a]
   b. (the following noun) [4.b]
5. (emphasizes the whole of the following phrase/entire following clause) [5]
6. (introduces a new, unsuspected moment/unexpected new development) [6]
7. (introduces the emphasized concluding sentence/ emphatic apodosis) [7]
8. (after verbs of perceiving) [8]
   - (of communicating/introducing announcement)
9. (הִנְנִי) [9]

  a. (with participle) [9.a]
  • (expression to announce a challenge)
  • (introduces certainty of being heard in prayer)
  b. (with 3rd. sg. imperfect) [9.b]
10. if (preceding a conditional clause) [10]

Arnold & Choi – exclamatory; immediacy; immediate perception; perception; logical, pp. 167–71 (§4.5); wish sentences, p. 203 (§5.3.3d)

BDB – pointing to persons or things; introducing clauses involving predication, making the narrative graphic and vivid for surprise or satisfaction; [conditional], pp. 243–44

DCH – introducing asseveration or strong affirmation; followed by question functioning as apodosis of conditional sentence, pp. 2:574–79

Gesenius – interjection, p. 307 (§105b); with participles, pp. 359–60 (§116p); incomplete sentence, pp. 469–70 (§147b)

Joüon & Muraoka – interjection, pp. 323–24 (§105d); *weqatal* (1cs) form (inverted perfect), p. 372 (§119n); asseverative clause, pp. 581–82 (§164a, g)

Van der Merwe – points to a newsworthy event or situation; points to noteworthy information; presentative; expressive; fixed expressions and specific contexts, pp. 407–18 (§40.22)

Waltke & O'Connor – describes immediate circumstances, present, or future time with participial clause, calling attention to a situation either for vividness or for its logical connection with some other event, pp. 625–28 (§37.6d–f); textual organization, p. 634 (§38.1e); presentative exclamations, pp. 675–78 (§30.2.1)

הַס (6x)/הַסּוּ (1x; Neh 8:11)

HALOT, p. 253; *Holladay*, p. 82

INTERJECTION
1. hush! keep silence!

BDB – interjection, p. 245
DCH – interjection, p. 2:579
Gesenius – interjection, p. 307 (§105a)
Joüon & Muraoka – cry for demanding silence, p. 322 (§105b)
Waltke & O'Connor – polite exclamation, p. 683 (§40.2.5c)

הַרְבֵּה (53x)

HALOT, p. 255; *Holladay*, p. 83

ADVERB
1. much, many, great number [substantive] [1]
   • (as subject)
   • (as object)
   • (as appositional)
   • (predicative)
2. very, much [degree] [2]
3. (with prepositions) [3]

Arnold & Choi – degree, p. 140 (§4.2.6)
BDB – adverb [of degree], p. 915
DCH – adverb [of degree], pp. 7:400–401
Gesenius – adverbial infinitive absolute [of degree], p. 295 (§100e)
Joüon & Muraoka – adverb [of degree], pp. 151, 490 (§§54d, 141h)
Van der Merwe – adverbial infinitive absolute of degree, pp. 183, 380 (§§20.2.4.2, 40.1.3.1c)
Waltke & O'Connor – adverb of degree, p. 659 (§39.3.1i)

וְ (50,270x)

HALOT, pp. 257–59; *Holladay*, pp. 84–85

CONJUNCTION

1. and (connecting 2 words or phrases) [conjunctive] [e.1]
   • (hendiadys)
2. (connecting 3 or more words) [conjunctive] [e.2]
3. also, even (emphasizing) [e.3]
4. with, and in addition (inclusive) [e.4]
5. and indeed; namely (explanatory) [e.5]
6. or (in conditional and interrogative clauses) [e.6]
7. (in repetition of a word, expresses disparity/variety) [e.7]
8. even so (following a word or phrase preceded by כְּ) [e.8]
9. וֹ . . . וֹ as well as, both . . . and [multiple inclusion] [e.9]
10. (connects two or more clauses) [conjunctive] [e.10]
11. (circumstantial clause beginning with וֹ represents a relative clause) [e.11]
12. (second clause beginning with וֹ adds adverbial phrases, supplementary explanations) [e.12]
13. (connecting imperatives and jussive) [e.13]
14. (connecting comparisons and parallelisms) [e.14]
15. but (contrastive) [e.15]
16. whether . . . or (alternative) [e.16]
17. as, while (conditions or circumstances) [e.17]
18. (taking up the subject of a main clause preceded by a clause of circumstance) [e.18]
19. although, therefore, because, etc. (introductory וֹ may often be translated by a conjunction other than "and") [conjunctive] [e.19]
20. (introducing a protestation/asseveration) [e.20]
21. in order that, that (after a command, question, or denial, וֹ before a jussive or cohortative expresses subordination) [purpose] [e.21]
22. so that (וֹ with imperative follows an imperative or jussive) [result] [e.22]
23. (introducing an apodosis after a conditional clause) [e.23]
   • (when the conditional clause is a *casus pendens*)

24. (pleonastic: when the conditional clause is a *casus pendens*) [e.24]
25. (introducing the verb after word of time) [e.25]
26. (introducing consequence/deductions or questions) [e.26]
27. and then (imperfect consecutive expresses the continuation of the action in narratives) [e.27]
    - (at the beginning of books)
    - so that (expression of conclusion/deduction)
    - although (adversative)
28. (expresses future in the perfect after imperfect, imperative, or jussive) [e.28]
    - (after expressions of time)
29. (other usages before perfect) [e.29]
    a. (iterative) [e.29.a]
    b. (Aramaism for imperfect consecutive) [e.29.b]
    c. (in style of official records/archival) [e.29.c]
30. (sustains the negation of לֹא and אַל, as though it were וְלֹא and וְאַל) [e.30]

Arnold & Choi – adversative; conjunctive; alternative; epexegetical; circumstantial; conditional; hendiadys, pp. 156–59 (§4.3.3); adversative clause, pp. 194–95 (§5.2.10); circumstantial clause, pp. 195–96 (§5.2.11); concessive clause, pp. 196–97 (§5.2.12)

BDB – [*conjunctive*]: [specifying]; explicative; exceeds or adds to what has preceded; alternative; contrastive; contrasted to suggest a question; attaching a fresh subject or object to a clause already grammatically complete; *waw* repeated; diversity or distribution; used in formulation of proverbs; concomitant conditions; *waw* consecutive; with a voluntative: intention; informal inference or consequence; introduces predicate or apodosis, pp. 251–55

DCH – [*conjunctive*]: in lists between each word or phrase;

[*waw* repeated]; linking repeated nouns in distributive structures; linking repeated nouns in a non-distributive structure; linking two words as representative parts of a whole; linking one word to another in a modifying role; disjunctive; [accompaniment]; [adversative]; [specifying]; explanatory, [pleonastic: when the conditional clause is a *casus pendens*]; [logical consequence]; [conditional/concessive]; [causal]; [purpose]; [comparative]; *waw* consecutive or conversive; [conditional]; redundant; [disjunctive: introducing new topic], pp. 2:596–98

Gesenius – sentences connected by *waw*, pp. 484–85 (§154); circumstantial clause, p. 489 (§156a, b); causal clause, p. 492 (§158a); consecutive clause, pp. 504–5 (§166a)

Joüon & Muraoka – with finite verbal forms, pp. 377–79 (§120); circumstantial clause, p. 566 (§159d); temporal clause, pp. 584–85 (§166a); conditional clause, p. 591 (§167b); final clause, p. 596 (§168b); consecutive clause, p. 598 (§169c); causal and explicative clause, p. 599 (§170c); adversative clause, pp. 602–3 (§172a); comparative clause, p. 605 (§174h); disjunctive clause, p. 605 (§175a); the *waw* of apodosis; syndesis and asyndesis, pp. 607–14 (§§176–177)

Van der Merwe – addition; "apparent" alternatives; coordination; fixed compound; correlative; superfluous; dislocated constituent; speech initial, hendiadys; diversity; contrastive; sequential; purpose; result; circumstance; motivation; background information; comparison; epexegetical or explicative, pp. 418–26 (§40.23)

Waltke & O'Connor – conjunctive; alternative; explicative; emphatic; relative; purpose, result; contrast; circumstance; comparison; interruptive (explanatory or parenthetical); epexegetical, pp. 648–54 (§39.2.1–5)

Williams – coordinative; hendiadys; verbal coordination; to join opposites; adversative; alternative; explicative;

pleonastic; accompaniment; comparative; emphatic; sarcastic; resumptive; adjunctive; distributive, pp. 152–56 (§§430a–442)

זו/זו/זה/זֶה (1178x)

HALOT, pp. 263–66; *Holladay*, pp. 86–87

DEMONSTRATIVE AND RELATIVE PRONOUN

1. this (is the one that), these (emphasizing) [1]
2. such (a one) [2]
3. this (זֶה in a neuter sense) [3]
4. this, that (זֹאת in a neuter sense) [4]
5. (אֵלֶּה ,זֹאת, זֶה anticipate what follows) [5]
6. (אֵלֶּה ,זֹאת, זֶה retroactively referring to what precedes) [6]
7. זֶה ... זֶה this ... that, one ... another, the one ... the other [7]
   - זֹאת ... זֹאת this one ... the other
8. (זֶה preceding a noun) [8]
9. (זֶה following a noun with suffix) [9]
10. (attributive אֵלֶּה ,זֹאת, זֶה following a noun with the article also have the article) [10]
11. the one from, he of, the (lord) of (זֶה with genitive) [11]
12. (זו/זו/זֶה introduces a relative clause like אֲשֶׁר) [12]
13. (adverb of place) [13]
    - בָּזֶה here
    - מִזֶּה away from here
    - מֵאֵת זֶה from there
    - מִזֶּה ... מִזֶּה on this side ... on that side
    - מִזֶּה וּמִזֶּה on either side
14. here, there (adverb of place) [14]
    - הַאַתָּה־זֶה is it you here?
    - וְהִנֵּה־זֶה and behold, there

- עַתָּה זֶה now, even now (with adverb of time)
- זֶה פַעֲמַיִם these two occasions
- זֶה כַמֶּה שָׁנִים for so many years now

15. (זֶה strengthens the interrogative) [15]
   - מַה־זֶּה how then?
   - מַה־זֹּאת and מַזֶּה what then?, לָמָּה זֶּה why then?, מִי הוּא זֶה who is this that. . .?, מִי זֹאת, מִי־זֶה and

16. (זֶה, זֹאת with prepositions) [16]
   a. בָּזֶה under these circumstances [16.a]
      - בְּזֹאת on this condition
      - בְּזֹאת on this occasion
      - בְּזֹאת for all this
      - בְּכָל־זֹאת and בְּכָל־זֶה for all this, on these conditions
   b. כָּזֶה such a one, such [16.b]
      - כָּזֹאת in this way, such a thing
      - כָּזֹאת in this (the same) way, as well
      - כָּזֹאת וְכָזֹאת this way and that, such and such
   c. with מִן [16.c]
   d. עַל־זֹאת for this reason, עַל־זֶה, עַל־אֵלֶּה this is why, because of all this [16.d]

Arnold & Choi – relative pronoun, p. 173 (§4.6.3)

BDB – demonstrative pronoun; in apposition to a substantive; as predicate; attached enclitically, almost as an adverb, to certain words, especially interrogative pronouns; in poetry, as a relative pronoun; with prefixes, pp. 260–62

DCH – demonstrative pronoun; predicate adjective or pronoun; combined relative pronoun with antecedent; relative pronoun; [with genitive]; attributive adjective; in combination with other words, pp. 3:82–89

Gesenius – adverb, p. 295 (§100f); demonstrative pronoun, pp. 442–43 (§136); interrogative pronoun, pp. 443, 473,

475–76 (§§137a, 150a, l); relative pronoun, pp. 446–47
(§138g); introduces independent relative clause, p. 447
(§138h); exclamations, p. 471 (§148b)

Joüon & Muraoka – demonstrative pronoun, pp. 498–501
(§143); relative pronoun, p. 504 (§145c)

Van der Merwe – introduces relative clause, p. 308 (§36.3.3);
adds emotional weight to a question, pp. 478, 480 (§§42.3.6,
42.3.8)

Waltke & O'Connor – simple demonstrative, pp. 310–12
(§137.4.2); *neutrum* pronoun, for a vague antecedent;
enclitic with exclamations; relative pronoun, pp. 312–13
(§17.4.3)

Williams – demonstrative as emphatic particle, p. 51 (§118);
relative pronoun, p. 54 (§129a)

זוּלַת/זוּלָה (16x)

HALOT, p. 267; *Holladay*, p. 87

PREPOSITION
  1. except, only, besides (after negation or question
  implying negation) [exceptive] [1]

CONJUNCTION
  1. save that, except that [exceptive] [2]

BDB – *preposition*: [exceptive]; *conjunction*: [exceptive],
  pp. 265–66
DCH – *preposition*: [exceptive], p. 3:97
Gesenius – [exceptive], p. 297 (§101a)

חוּץ (164x)

HALOT, p. 298; *Holladay*, p. 98

ADVERB

1. outside [spatial] [1]
2. חוּצָה(הַ) outside [substantive] [2]
3. (with prepositions) [3]
   a. בַּחוּץ out of doors [3.a]
   b. לַחוּצָה on the outside, לַחוּץ לְ on the outside [3.b]
   c. אֶל־הַחוּץ, from inside to out [3.c]
   d. מִן הַחוּץ those outside [3.d]
      - מִחוּץ from outside, on the outside, outside
      - מִחוּץ לְ, מֵחוּץ, and מִחוּצָה לְ on the outside of
      - אֶל־מִחוּץ לְ to the outside of
4. חוּץ מִן except [4]

BDB – [*substantive*]; [*adverb*]: [spatial], pp. 299–300
DCH – [*substantive*]; *adverb*: [spatial]; *preposition*: [spatial], pp. 3:175–77
Waltke & O'Connor – adverb of location, p. 658 (§39.3.1g)

חִישׁ (1x; Ps 90:10)

HALOT, p. 313; *Holladay*, p. 103

ADVERB

1. quickly, in haste [manner]

BDB – *adverb* [of manner], p. 301
DCH – *adverb* [of manner], p. 3:217

חָלִילָה (21x)

see II חָלִיל in *HALOT*, pp. 318–19; *Holladay*, p. 105

INTERJECTION

1. far be it from (aversive/preventative, negative interjection) [1]
   a. (with לְ) [1.a]
      - חָלִילָה חָלִילָה לִי (with explicative)
      - (followed by an oath with אִם)
   b. that I (or he) should do (with מִן and infinitive) [1.b]
   c. to do (with לְ and infinitive) [1.c]
2. חָלִילָה strengthened by מִן + Yhwh [2]
   a. חָלִילָה לִי מֵיהוָה the LORD forbid!/far be it from me before (in the presence of) Yhwh [2.a]
   b. that I (or he) should do (with מִן and infinitive) [2.b]

BDB – exclamation; + מִן and infinitive of act deprecated, p. 321

DCH – negative interjection, pp. 3:232–33

Gesenius – interjection, p. 307 (§105b); sentences which express an oath or asseveration, pp. 471–72 (§149a, e)

Joüon & Muraoka – clause of curse and oath, p. 584 (§165k)

Van der Merwe – refusal to accept a state of affairs; to distance the speaker from a situation or action, pp. 484–85 (§44.8)

Waltke & O'Connor – oath and wish exclamation, p. 680 (§40.2.2c); nominal exclamation, p. 681 (§40.2.3b)

חִנָּם (32x)

HALOT, p. 334; *Holladay*, p. 110

ADVERB

1. without giving or taking compensation [manner] [1]
2. for nothing = in vain [manner] [2]
3. without cause, undeservedly [manner] [3]

BDB – *substantive; adverbial accusative*, p. 336

DCH – *adverb*; [substantive], pp. 3:271–72
Gesenius – adverb [of manner], p. 295 (§100g)
Joüon & Muraoka – derived adverb, p. 303n2 (§102b)
Van der Merwe – adverb of manner, pp. 381–82 (§40.1.3.1.1b)
Waltke & O'Connor – manner adverb, p. 659 (§39.3.1j)

חֶרֶשׁ (1x; Josh 2:1)

see II חֶרֶשׁ in *HALOT*, p. 358; *Holladay*, p. 118

ADVERB
> 1. very quietly, secretly [manner]

BDB – *adverb*, p. 361
DCH – *adverb*, p. 3:325
Waltke & O'Connor – manner adverb, p. 659 (§39.3.1j)

טְרוֹם (alternative form of טֶרֶם) (1x; Ruth 3:14)

HALOT, p. 379; *Holladay*, p. 125

CONJUNCTION
> 1. even before [temporal]

BDB – *adverb*: [temporal], p. 382
DCH – *conjunction*: [temporal], pp. 3:374–75

טֶרֶם (56x)

HALOT, pp. 379–80; *Holladay*, p. 125

CONJUNCTION/PREPOSITION
> 1. not yet [temporal] [1]
>   a. with perfect [1.a]

b. with imperfect [1.b]
2. (even) before [temporal] [2]
3. בְּטֶרֶם [temporal] [3]
   a. before (preposition) [3.a]
   b. before with perfect (always passive) (conjunction) [3.b]
      • with imperfect
      • with pleonastic לֹא
4. even before (מִטֶּרֶם with infinitive) [4]

Arnold & Choi – later or succeeding situation in a temporal clause, p. 190 (§5.2.4b)

BDB – adverb of time, p. 382

DCH – [temporal], pp. 3:374–76

Gesenius – use of the imperfect, pp. 314–15 (§107c); negative sentence, pp. 478, 481 (§152a, r); temporal clause, p. 502 (§164c)

Joüon & Muraoka – conjunction, p. 319 (§104b); *yiqtol* form (future), p. 342 (§113j); negative clause, p. 572 (§160n)

Van der Merwe – sentential negative; a point in time prior to the referent, pp. 462–63 (§41.8)

Waltke & O'Connor – temporal clause, pp. 514, 643 (§§31.6.3c, 38.7a); temporal adverb, p. 658 (§39.3.1h)

Williams – temporal clause, p. 180 (§509)

יוֹמָם (50x)

HALOT, pp. 401–2; *Holladay*, p. 131

ADVERB
1. the same as יוֹם [substantive] [1]
2. during the day, by day [temporal] [2]

Arnold & Choi – temporal locative, p. 146 (§4.2.7)

BDB – *substantive*; *adverb*: [temporal], p. 401
DCH – *adverb*: [temporal], p. 4:186
Gesenius – adverb [temporal], p. 295 (§100g)
Joüon & Muraoka – adverb [temporal], p. 303 (§102b)
Van der Merwe – temporal adverb, p. 380 (§40.1.3.1b)
Waltke & O'Connor – temporal adverb, p. 658 (§39.3.1h)
Williams – adverb [temporal], p. 137 (§377)

יֶתֶר/יוֹתֵר (9x)

HALOT, p. 404; *Holladay*, p. 132

ADVERB

1. the rest, what remains, is left over [substantive; only 1 Sam 15:15] [1]
2. too much, excessively, so very, extremely [degree] [2]
3. (with prepositions) [3]
    a. with לְ, advantage [3.a]
    b. with מִן, more than [3.b]
    c. with שֶׁ, not to mention that [3.c]

BDB – [*substantive*]; *adverb*: [degree], p. 452
DCH – [*substantive*]; *adverb*: [degree], p. 4:193
Joüon & Muraoka – [degree], p. 489n2 (§141g)
Waltke & O'Connor – adverb of degree, p. 659 (§39.3.1i)

יַחַד (47x)

HALOT, pp. 405–6; *Holladay*, p. 132

ADVERB

1. uniting, union, association, community (substantive) [1]
2. (= יַחְדָּו) [2]

a. together, all at once, with each other, altogether (preceding verb) [2.a]
b. altogether, with each other (following verb) [2.b]

BDB – *substantive*; *adverbial accusative*, p. 403
DCH – [*substantive*]; *adverb*: proximity or unity; inclusiveness of entirety; exclusivity; degree; time; association, pp. 4:195–98
Joüon & Muraoka – adverbial accusative, pp. 304–5 (§102d)
Waltke & O'Connor – manner adverb, p. 659 (§39.3.1j)

יַחְדָּו (96x)

HALOT, p. 406; *Holladay*, p. 132

ADVERB

1. together, with each other, altogether, equally likewise (preceding verb) [1]
2. together, altogether, at the same time (following verb) [2]

BDB – of community in action; emphatic; alikeness, p. 403
DCH – proximity or unity; inclusiveness or entirety; exclusivity; degree; association; activity, p. 4:198
Joüon & Muraoka – adverbial accusative, pp. 304–5 (§102d)
Waltke & O'Connor – manner adverb, p. 659 (§39.3.1j)

יָמִין (139x)

see I יָמִין in *HALOT*, p. 415; *Holladay*, p. 136

ADVERB

1. right side [substantive] [1]
2. הַיָּמִין to the right, מִימִין right of, עַל־יְמִינוֹ on his

right, לִימִינְךָ at your right side, לַיָּמִין to the right [spatial] [2]

3. regarded highly, particularly valued [metaphorical] [3]
4. the right side as the south side [substantive] [4]

BDB – [*substantive*], p. 411
DCH – [*substantive*], pp. 4:227–29

יַעַן (99x)

HALOT, p. 421; Holladay, p. 138

PREPOSITION

    1. because of [causal] [1]
        a. with substantive [1.a]
        b. with infinitive [1.b]
        c. יַעַן מֶה why? [1.c]

CONJUNCTION

    1. because [causal] [2]
        a. with perfect [2.a]
        b. (יַעַן אֲשֶׁר) [2.b]
        c. (יַעַן כִּי) [2.c]
        d. יַעַן (וּ)בְיַעַן therefore because (with infinitive; with perfect) [2.d]

Arnold & Choi – causal, pp. 122, 191–92 (§§4.1.8, 5.2.5)
BDB – *preposition*: causal; *conjunction*: causal, pp. 774–75
DCH – *conjunction*: causal; *preposition*: [casual], pp. 4:223–24
Gesenius – causal clause, p. 492 (§158b)
Hardy – causal, p. 94 (§3.7.2)
Joüon & Muraoka – causal and explicative clauses, pp. 599–600 (§170f)
Van der Merwe – grounds, p. 440 (§40.35)

Waltke & O'Connor – causal clause, pp. 202, 640 (§§11.2.8, 38.4a)

Williams – causal, pp. 133–34 (§363a–b)

יֵשׁ (138x)

HALOT, pp. 443–44; *Holladay*, pp. 145–46

PARTICLE
1. what is in existence: property (substantive) [1]
2. it exists, there is [existence] [2]
3. (with preceding substantive) [3]
   a. (absolute) [3.a]
   b. with (אֵת or עִם) [3.b]
   c. יֵשׁ אֶת־נַפְשְׁכֶם you are willing (neutral) [3.c]
4. there are those who, meaning: many (with participle) [4]
5. (with suffix as subject + participle) (equivalent to "copula") [5]
6. (יֵשׁ לְ dative of possession) [6]
   a. יֵשׁ לוֹ he possesses [6.a]
   b. (I) have to, should (לְ with infinitive) [6.b]
   c. (with negative) [6.c]
7. (יֵשׁ with adverb of place) [7]
   a. here is (with פֹּה) [7.a]
   b. in, on (with בְּ) [7.b]
   c. in the place of, under (with תַּחַת) [7.c]

Arnold & Choi – existence; possession; predicate, p. 167 (§4.4.2); existential sentence for present time, p. 203 (§5.3.4b)

BDB – substance; existence, pp. 441–42

DCH – linking subject to a complement, or as the complement of an indefinite subject; [*substantive*]; [conditional: יֵשׁ אֲשֶׁר], pp. 4:315–17

Gesenius – existence in conditional and interrogative sentences, p. 454 (§141k)

Joüon & Muraoka – existence in a place (presence); existence as such, pp. 541–42 (§154k)

Van der Merwe – expresses existence of an undetermined entity; affirms the presence or involvement of an identifiable entity in a situation, pp. 482–83 (§43.3)

Waltke & O'Connor – particles denoting existence, p. 72 (§10.3.2b)

Williams – as a noun; existence; possession; before the pronominal subject of a participle; obligation; elliptic, pp. 170–71 (§§476–481)

יֶתֶר (95x)

see I יֶתֶר in *HALOT*, p. 452; *Holladay*, p. 148

ADVERB
1. rest, what is left behind [substantive] [1]
2. rest, remainder [substantive] [2]
3. excessively [manner] [3]
   - גָּדוֹל יֶתֶר מְאֹד very great indeed
   - עַל־יֶתֶר exceedingly

BDB – [*substantive*]; in adverbial phrases, pp. 451–52
DCH – [*substantive*], pp. 4:344–45

כְּ (2,900x)

HALOT, pp. 453–54; *Holladay*, p. 149

PREPOSITION
1. (expressing identity) [1]
   a. like, as [1.a]

b. with כְּ twice [1.b]
  - (the subject in question comes first) [1.b.i]
  - (the thing to which something is compared comes first) [1.b.ii]
2. (conformity of measure) [2]
   a. as many as [2.a]
   b. [develops into] about (=approximately) [2.b]
3. in the same way as, of the same sort as (conformity/agreement of kind) [3]
   - [develops into] according to, after, suitable to
4. (with various prepositions) [4]
   a. (are sometimes included in כְּ) [4.a]
   b. (otherwise, in fixed expressions) [4.b]
5. (seemingly superfluous, stressing/accentuating, pleonastic, confirmatory, כְּ *veritatis*) [5]
6. = "something like" (stylistic feature of visions) [6]
7. (preceding infinitive) (= כַּאֲשֶׁר with finite verb) [7]
   a. as (comparative) [7.a]
   b. when, as soon as (temporal) [7.b]

Arnold & Choi – agreement; correspondence; temporal, pp. 122–23 (§4.1.9); comparative clause, p. 193 (§5.2.6b)
BDB – to express exact or approximate equality; to express resemblance in respect of some attribute, action, character, appearance, etc.; accusative of mode or limitation: conformity to a standard or rule, comparative; comparative of class or correspondence with an idea; to signify the completeness of the correspondence between two objects; comparative or temporal before an infinitive, pp. 453–55
DCH – comparative; special cases of comparison: approximation, of unattainables, uniqueness, idealization, inequality, or [with demonstrative]; equivalence; approximate number; [in accordance with/according to]; [temporal]; possessive, pp. 4:347–48

Gesenius – manner; time; *kaph veritatis*, pp. 375–76 (§188s–x); comparative clause, p. 499 (§161c)

Joüon & Muraoka – perfect similitude; imperfect similitude; temporal, p. 461 (§133g); temporal clause, pp. 588–89 (§166.l, m); comparative clause, p. 604 (§174c)

Van der Merwe – similarity; comparability; quantitative agreement; proximity in time, pp. 345–47 (§39.10)

Waltke & O'Connor – agreement in quantity or measure; approximations; agreement in kind; agreement in manner or norm; correspondence (or identity); *kaph veritatis*; emphatic; temporal, pp. 202–5 (§11.2.9); nominal uses of infinitive construct with prepositions, p. 604 (§36.2.2b)

Williams – likeness; comparative; approximation; concessive; norm; asseverative; temporal; pregnant, pp. 101–4 (§§255–264)

כַּאֲשֶׁר (510x)

HALOT, p. 455; *Holladay*, pp. 149–50

PREPOSITION

    1. as, according as [in accordance with/according to] [1]
        a. exactly as (enhancing) [1.a]
        b. (elliptical: the verb is not repeated) [1.b]
        c. (in expression of resignation/submission) [1.c]
        d. כַּאֲשֶׁר ... כֵּן as ... so, the more ... the more [1.d]
    2. therefore that = because (causal) [2]
    3. supposing, as though (hypothetical) [3]
    4. (temporal) [4]
        a. as = when (with perfect) [4.a]
        b. after (pleonastic) [4.b]
        c. when (with imperfect) [4.c]

Arnold & Choi – contemporary action or situation, p. 189 (§5.2.4a); comparative clause, pp. 192–93 (§5.2.6a)

BDB – [in accordance with/according to]; causal; temporal, p. 455

DCH – comparative; temporal; conditional; causal; [independent relative]; introducing noun, not clause, pp. 1:434–35

Gesenius – comparative clause, p. 499 (§151b)

Joüon & Muraoka – causal and explicative clause, p. 601 (§170k); comparative clause, p. 604 (§174a)

Van der Merwe – similarity; quantitative agreement; temporal, pp. 345–47 (§39.10)

Waltke & O'Connor – comparative clause, p. 641 (§38.5a); temporal clause, p. 643 (§38.7)

Williams – causal; temporal; comparison, pp. 102–4 (§§260, 262b, 264)

כְּבָר (9x)

see I כְּבָר in *HALOT*, p. 459; *Holladay*, p. 151

ADVERB

  1. already [temporal]

BDB – [temporal], p. 460
DCH – [temporal], p. 4:359
Gesenius – adverbial accusative [of time], pp. 294–95 (§100c)
Waltke & O'Connor – temporal adverb, p. 658 (§39.3.1h)

כֹּה (577x)

HALOT, p. 461; *Holladay*, p. 152

ADVERB

  1. here (locative) [1]

2. now (temporal) [2]

3. thus, so [manner] [3]

    a. as (said/done) before [3.a]

    b. as follows [3.b]

    c. כֹּה אָמַר thus says (introducing a messenger's word) [3.c]

        • (profane = without divine name) [3.c.i]

        • [3.c.ii] (כֹּה אָמַר יְהוָה)

4. (כֹּה repeated) [4]

Arnold & Choi – manner; demonstrative/locative, pp. 146–47 (§4.2.8)

BDB – manner; place; time, p. 462

DCH – manner; place or direction; compounds, pp. 4:362–63

Joüon & Muraoka – demonstrative adverb, p. 306 (§102h)

Van der Merwe – introduces direct speech; oath; anaphoric adverb; proximate location; proximate point in time, pp. 431–32 (§40.28)

Waltke & O'Connor – adverb of location, p. 658 (§39.3.1g); emphatic adverb, p. 665 (§39.3.4e)

כִּי (4,483x)

see II כִּי in *HALOT*, pp. 470–71; *Holladay*, pp. 155–56

DEMONSTRATIVE PARTICLE

    1. (emphatic, deictic/corroborative, stressing/strengthening) [A.1]

        a. yes, indeed, certainly [A.1.a]

        b. truly, indeed (introducing positive oath clause) (כִּי אִם) [A.1.b]

    2. (introduces conclusion) [A.2]

        a. (conclusion after condition-clause introduced by לֹא אִם) [A.2.a]

    b. (introduces conclusion after a condition
       introduced by לוּלֵא/יְ) [A.2.b]
       • (introduced by לֵא or לוּ)
       • (introduced by אִם)
    c. (כִּי עַתָּה when the preceding condition is only
       supposed/implied) [A.2.c]
  3. (following a negative clause) [A.3]
    a. on the contrary, only [adversative] [A.3.a]
    b. (in protestations/contradicting reply) [A.3.b]
       • no, but, on the contrary (לֹא כִּי) [A.3.b.i]
       • no! not thus! (לֹא כִי) (without dagesh lene)
       [A.3.b.ii]
    c. no, on the contrary (preceding negation only
       implied) [A.3.c]
  4. but, except [exceptive] [A.4]
  5. but would he really . . . ? (in an objection raised by
    the speaker) (כִּי אִם) [A.5]

CONJUNCTION
  1. because (causal clause before main clause) [B.1]
  2. for (causal clause after main clause) [B.2]
  3. for this reason (a reason, long in existence, is finally
    recognized) [B.3]
    • (as formula of politeness)
  4. (combinations) [B.4]
    a. (כִּ may be separated from its clause by an אִם
       clause) [B.4.a]
    b. הֲכִי is it true that? [B.4.b]
       • (הֲכִי implying a positive answer)
       • (הֲלֹא כִי implying a positive answer)
    c. it is true, is it not, that . . . ? (וְכִי introducing a
       rhetorical question) [B.4.c]
    d. (see אַף כִּי) [B.4.d]
    e. only (אַךְ כִּי) [B.4.e]

5. that (introduces an object-clause after verb of seeing, hearing, saying, knowing, believing, remembering, forgetting, rejoicing, regretting, etc.) [nominalizing] [B.5]
6. (object of the main clause is identical with the subject of the sub-ordinate clause) [nominalizing] [B.6]
   - (reinforced by הִיא, הוּא)
   - (same transposition/anticipation with time-phrase, i.e., "I know after my death that" = "I know that after my death" [Deut 31:29])
     - (כִּי separated from governing verb)
     - (the subject of the clause introduced with כִּי becomes the genitive of the object in the governing clause)
7. (introducing direct discourse, like ὅτι) [B.7]
8. [B.8] (תַּחַת כִּי, עֵקֶב כִּי, עַל־כִּי, עַד־כִּי, יַעַן כִּי, אֶפֶס כִּי)
9. (after a main clause which is negative or interrogative, introduces a subordinate clause which explains/defines and fulfils/amplifies the idea of the principle clause) [explanatory/amplification] [B.9]
10. when (almost = if) (temporal) [B.10]
    - (the subject may precede כִּי)
11. if, in case (conditional) [B.11]
12. although, even though (concessive) [B.12]
13. as (modal) [B.13]
14. that [purpose] [B.14]

Arnold & Choi – causal; evidential; clarification; result; temporal; conditional; adversative; concessive; asseverative; perceptual; subject; recitative; exceptive; interrogative, pp. 160–66 (§4.3.4); substantival clause, pp. 185–86 (§5.2.1a, c); real conditional clause, p. 187 (§5.2.2a); result clause, p. 188 (§5.2.3b); temporal clause, pp. 189–90 (§5.2.4a, b); causal clause, pp. 191–92 (§5.2.5); exceptive clause, p. 193 (§5.2.7); adversative clause, pp. 194–95 (§5.2.10); concessive clause, pp. 196–97 (§5.2.12); oath sentence, pp. 201–2 (§5.3.2)

BDB – [nominalizing]; introduces direct narration; oath; adding force or distinctiveness to an affirmation; intensive; expressing consecution; added to prepositions; temporal; [conditional]; concessive; [causal], pp. 471–75

DCH – causal; [nominalizing]; relative; purpose; conditional or temporal; concessive; introducing apodosis; adversative; emphatic; consequence; [comparative], as interrogative particle or pronoun; [preposition: concessive/causal]; in other compounds, pp. 4:383–91

Gesenius – exclamation, p. 471 (§148d); oath or asseveration (§149); negative sentence, p. 479 (§152c); object-clause, p. 492 (§157b); causal clause, p. 492 (§158b); conditional sentence, pp. 494–98 (§159l, z, aa, bb, ee); concessive clause, p. 498 (§160b); disjunctive sentence, p. 500 (§162a); adversative and exceptive clause, p. 500 (§163); temporal clause, p. 502 (§164d); consecutive clause, p. 505 (§166b).

Joüon & Muraoka – nominal clause, pp. 532–33 (§154fa); interrogative sentence, p. 576 (§161i); asseverative clause, pp. 581–82 (§164b, c, g); clause of curse and oath, pp. 582–83 (§165b, e); temporal clause, p. 589 (§166o); conditional clause, pp. 591–95 (§167); consecutive clause (§169e); causal and explicative clause, pp. 599–601 (§170); concessive clause, pp. 601–2 (§171); adversative clause, p. 603 (§172c); exceptive clause, p. 603 (§173)

Van der Merwe – introduces protasis of a condition; temporal, cause of a condition or process; complementizer; causal grounds; counter-statement after a negative statement; oath, pp. 432–36 (§40.29)

Waltke & O'Connor – particles expressing contingency, p. 510 (§31.6.1); conditional clause, pp. 637–38 (§38.2d, e); final and result clauses, pp. 638–39 (§38.3b); causal clause, pp. 640–41 (§38.4a); exceptive clause, pp. 642–43 (§38.6b); temporal clause, pp. 643–44 (§38.7a); constituent noun clause, pp. 644–46 (§38.8); emphatic adverb,

pp. 663–67 (§39.3.4c–e); restrictive adverb, pp. 670–71
(§39.3.5d); oath and wish exclamation, pp. 679–80
(§40.2.2b)

Williams – causal; temporal; conditional; adversative;
concessive; asseverative; result; nominalizing; question;
recitative, pp. 156–59 (§§444–452)

כִּי אִם־/כִּי־אִם (154x)

HALOT, p. 471; *Holladay*, p. 156

CONJUNCTION

A. כִּי and אִם introduce two clauses independent of
each other [A]

B. כִּי and אִם form a logical unit (approx. 140 times) [B]

1. (emphasizing/affirmative particle) [B.1]
   a. but, nevertheless, yet, actually [B.1.a]
   b. surely, truly (introducing a positive oath-clause) [B.1.b]
2. (particle expressing exception after a negative) [B.2]
   a. but (rather) [B.2.a]
   b. unless, except [B.2.b]
      - unless, except if (before a clause) [B.2.b.i]
      - except, but (before a noun) [B.2.b.ii]
      - מִי ... כִּי אִם who is ... if not/except;
        מַה ... כִּי אִם what ... except = nothing
        but [B.2.b.iii]

Arnold & Choi – exceptive clause, p. 193 (§5.2.7); adversative clause, p. 194 (§5.2.10); concessive clause, pp. 196–97 (§5.2.12)

BDB – each particle retaining its independent force, relating to a different clause; the two particles being closely conjoined, relating to the same clause: limiting; pleonastic

אִם, contradiction of the previous clause; after an oath, strengthened כִּי, introducing the fact sworn to, p. 474

DCH – [adversative]; [exceptive]; [contrastive: otherwise]; oath and asseveration; [each particle retaining its independent force], pp. 4:389–90

Joüon & Muraoka – asseverative clause, p. 582 (§163c); clause of curse and oath, pp. 582–83 (§165c, e); adversative clause, p. 603 (§172c); exceptive clause, p. 603 (§173b)

Van der Merwe – alternative, p. 436 (§40.21.2)

Waltke & O'Connor – exceptive clause, pp. 642–43 (§38.6.b); restrictive adverb, p. 671 (§39.3.5.d); oath and wish exclamation, p. 679 (§40.2.2.b)

Williams – adversative, pp. 157, 196 (§§447, 555); asseverative, p. 158 (§449); exceptive, p. 197 (§556)

כָּלִיל (1x; Isa 2:18)

HALOT, p. 479; *Holladay*, p. 159

ADVERB

1. completely [degree] [1.c]

BDB – [substantive]; *adverbial accusative*, p. 483
DCH – *adjective*; *adverb* [of degree], p. 4:425

כַּמֶה/כַּמָה (13x)

see מָה in *HALOT*, p. 551; *Holladay*, p. 184

PREPOSITION

1. how much? how many? how few? how often? [interrogative] [D.2]

BDB – [interrogative of quantity], pp. 553–54

DCH – [interrogative of quantity], p. 5:160

Gesenius – interrogative, p. 113 (§37e); double questions, p. 475 (§150h)

Joüon & Muraoka – interrogative, p. 107 (§37d)

Waltke & O'Connor – interrogative, p. 325 (§18.3d)

כֵּן (550x)

see II כֵּן in *HALOT*, pp. 482–83; *Holladay*, pp. 159–60

ADVERB

1. thus, so (= as has just been said) [in accordance with/according to] [1]
2. thus, so (= as is now to be said) [in accordance with/according to] [2]
3. in the same manner, just the same way, just so [manner] [3]
4. so (in various extended meanings) [4]
   - = therefore, that is why [inference]
   - = so much [quantity]
   - = something like it [approximation]
   - לֹא כֵן not thus ! (preventive)
5. as . . . so [comparative] [5]
   a. (כְּ . . . כֵּן) [5.a]
      - (temporal)
   b. (כַּאֲשֶׁר . . . כֵּן) [5.b]
   c. (כְּמוֹ . . . כֵּן) [5.c]
6. just as . . . so (כְּכֹל אֲשֶׁר . . . כֵּן ,כְּכֹל . . . כֵּן) [comparative] [6]
7. thus . . . as, so . . . as [comparative] [7]
   a. (כֵּן . . . כְּ) [7.a]
   b. (כֵּן . . . כַּאֲשֶׁר) [7.b]
8. then (temporal) [8]
   a. so, as well, also (unstressed) [8.a]

    b. אַחֲרֵי־כֵן afterwards [8.b]

    c. בְּכֵן thereupon, so then [8.c]

    d. עַד־כֵן as yet, until then [8.d]

9. (miscellaneous, with various other words) [9]

    a. (see עַל־כֵן and לָכֵן) [9.a]

    b. (לֹא כֵן = לָכֵן) (textual error? e.g., genitive 4:15) [9.b]

    c. (כֵּן . . . וְכֵן) (continuation) [9.c]

Arnold & Choi – comparative; manner; compounds, pp. 147–48, 192–93 (§§4.2.10, 5.2.6)

BDB – manner; quantity; quality; degree; often, to emphasize the agreement, in answer to כְּ, and כַּאֲשֶׁר; compounds, pp. 485–87

DCH – manner; quantity; temporal; [additive]; [comparative]; apparently as a preposition; compounded with preceding preposition, pp. 4:429–34

Gesenius – comparative clause, p. 499 (§161b, c)

Joüon & Muraoka – demonstrative adverb, p. 306 (§102h); causal and explicative clause, p. 599 (§170h); comparative clause, p. 604 (§174b)

Van der Merwe – correspondence of behavioral mode or discourse active action; event or state of affairs; accordance of quality of entities to a positive norm, p. 437 (§40.30)

Waltke & O'Connor – comparative clause, p. 641 (§38.5a); emphatic adverb, p. 663 (§39.3.4c, d, e)

Williams – comparison, p. 104 (§264)

לְ (20,062x)

see I לְ in *HALOT*, pp. 507–10; *Holladay*, pp. 167–69

PREPOSITION

1. to, toward (spatial/locative) [1]

    • (movement in a given direction) [directional]

2. to (purpose, aim of movement: expressing arrival at destination) [terminative] [2]
3. (temporal) [3]
   a. until [3.a]
   b. at, in [3.b]
      - when (with infinitive)
   c. for a time [develops into] for a duration [3.c]
4. to, toward (direction, no physical movement) [metaphorical] [4]
5. away from (= מִן) [ablative] [5]
   - more than (comparative) (this usage is questionable; e.g., Nah 1:7)
6. of, about (with verbs of speaking) [specification] [6]
7. into, to be (aim, purpose of an action) [7]
   - (office or station to which someone is appointed)
   - (make someone something)
   - (material or object into which something is made)
8. (dative of advantage or disadvantage) [8]
   a. good with regard to = good for, an advantage to him [8.a]
   b. for = against [8.b]
   c. in the interest of, in favor of [8.c]
9. *often untranslated* (ethical dative, of interest: personal reference same as subject of verb, emphasizing the interest or share the subject has in that action) [9]
10. belonging to, with (belonging to a given party, group, leader) [10]
11. have, belongs to (dative of possession) [11]
12. (prepared) for, with (= in the power of) (readiness/ preparation, availability/disposition, competence/ fitness) [12]
13. become, into, to (result or product) [13]
14. of (genitive-relationship for indefinite nouns) [14]
15. (stands for/replaces genitive) [15]

- (with indeterminate noun)
- (in place of second genitive)

16. (reinforces a preposition) [16]

17. (expressing with a noun an adverbial phrase of situation, manner) [17]

18. (distributive) [18]
- every (repeated singular)
- each (with plural)

19. (specification: expresses that in respect to which something is affirmed) [19]
a. concerning, in (regard to) [19.a]
b. [develops into] than (comparative) [19.b]

20. according to, by (indicates the composition of the whole by sections) [partitive] [20]

21. in relation to, in the direction of, or *untranslated* (may introduce the logical direct object, usually personal/expresses an accusative) [21]

22. namely (apposition) [22]

23. for, because (cause or motive) [23]

24. by [agency] [24]

25. *untranslated* (inscriptions, titles) [25]

Arnold & Choi – spatial; locative; temporal; purpose; quasidatival (interest/advantage, product); possession; genitival; specification; normative; manner; estimative; agent; reflexive, pp. 123–28 (§4.1.10)

BDB – direction; locality; denotes object of a verb; transition into a new state or condition, or into a new character or office; reference: relation, possession, periphrastic for the construct state, attached to adverbs it forms prepositions, agency, [specification], cause or occasion, aim, object, or consequence, reflexive (ethical dative), norm or standard, condition or state; time, with infinitive, pp. 510–17

DCH – possession; direction; [state/function/capacity];

place; purpose; relation; benefit; reflexive; [in accordance
with/according to]; specifying or emphasizing; [quan-
tity]; introducing object; agency; causal; accompaniment;
instrument; estimation; [disadvantage: hostility]; privative; asseverative or emphatic; vocative; direction; with
infinitive construct, pp. 4:479–85

Gesenius – direction toward; varied relations of an action or
state; periphrasis for the *genetivus possessoris* or *auctoris*
[i.e., genitive of possessor or author or cause]; locative;
temporal; distributive; *nota dativi* [i.e., sign of the dative];
dativus commodi (or *incommodi*) [i.e., dative of advantaged or disadvantaged person]; result; specification;
inscription or title, pp. 381–82 (§119r–u)

Joüon & Muraoka – genitive replaced by לְ, pp. 445–48
(§130); of relation, p. 455 (§132f); direction; as accusative;
possession; as genitive; causality; finality and yardstick;
temporal; *dativus commodi* and *incommodi* [i.e., dative
of advantaged or disadvantaged person]; with verbs of
motion, p. 458 (§133d); numerals, p. 496 (§142p)

Van der Merwe – indirect object relationship; signals a hearer
with verbs of saying; experienced relationship; marks
direct object; marks an experiencing person or thing in
a non-causative way; reclassification; re-identification:
whole/part; re-identification: principle of division; actu-
alization (ethical dative); spatial; directional; locational;
temporal; distributional; circumstance; norm; purpose;
result; causal, pp. 348–57 (§39.11)

Waltke & O'Connor – locative; temporal; transformation;
purpose; as marking direct object, pp. 183–85 (§10.4); spatial; temporal; allative spatial; interest or (dis)advantage;
ethical dative; indirect object; possessive; specification;
apposition; emphatic, pp. 205–12 (§11.2.10)

Williams – spatially terminative; temporally terminative;
direction; temporal point; temporal duration; indirect

object; possessive; advantage; disadvantage; reflexive; specification; direct object; subject of a passive verb; in place of a repeated preposition; manner; comparison; purpose; product; result; agent; distributive; partisanship; asseverative; obligation, pp. 105–12 (§§265–284)

לְ + infinitive construct (4,486x)

see I לְ in *HALOT*, entry 26, p. 510; *Holladay*, p. 169

[PREPOSITION INTRODUCING AN INFINITIVE]
1. in order to (intention/purpose) [26.a]
2. (completion of incomplete verbal ideas) [nominal accusative: verbal complement] [26.b]
3. (a more precise determination of the governing verb translated adverbially) [nominal accusative: adverbial accusative] [26.c]
4. (accompanying circumstance) [specification] [26.d]
5. (הָיָה with infinitive with לְ) [26.e]
6. (after יֵשׁ) [26.f]
7. (לֹא and infinitive) [26.g]
8. should (לְ with infinitive as verb of an independent clause, which states that something will, should or must happen) [obligation] [26.h]
9. in, toward (temporal) [26.i]

Arnold & Choi – infinitive construct, pp. 83–85 (§3.4.1c, d, f, g); substantival nominative clause, p. 185 (§5.2.1a); final clause, p. 187 (§5.2.3); causal clause, p. 191 (§5.2.5)
BDB – purpose; limiting or qualifying idea expressed by principal verb, pp. 517–18
DCH – [purpose]; following modal or auxiliary verb; with verb of quantity or quality; ability or sufficiency; [nominal]; introducing object clause, pp. 4:484–85

Gesenius – the infinitive, p. 123 (§45f, g); the infinitive construct, pp. 348–52 (§114); final clause, p. 504 (§165c)

Joüon & Muraoka – the infinitive construct, pp. 405–8 (§124l–p)

Van der Merwe – infinitive construct, pp. 172–76 (§20.1); nominal; purpose; explicative; consequence, pp. 350–53 (§39.11.3)

Waltke & O'Connor – infinitive construct with the preposition לְ, pp. 605–10 (§36.2.3)

Williams – degree; subject or direct object; purpose; result, pp. 109–10 (§§275–277, 279)

לֹא (5,167x)

HALOT, pp. 511–12; *Holladay*, p. 170

NEGATIVE PARTICLE

1. not, un- (factual, stated negation) [1]
2. (prohibition) [2]
   a. shall not (with imperfect may express unconditional prohibition) [2.a]
   b. you may not (rarely with jussive) [2.b]
3. no, not (negates a single word in the clause) [3]
   • none at all, nothing at all (with emphasis)
4. not (negates nominal clause) [4]
5. (לֹא and following word make up the whole clause) [5]
6. (negates two consecutive verbs) [6]
7. so that not, in order that not (introduces subordinate clause) [7]
8. (circumstantial clause before a substantive) [8]
   a. without (adverbial) [8.a]
   b. without, -less (appositionally in a negative description) [8.b]
9. (לֹא and וְלֹא = הֲלֹא and וַהֲלֹא if the context of a question is already clear) [9]
10. no (in answer to question) [10]

- לֹא כִי no, rather
11. (אִם לֹא) [11]
    a. (whether) . . . or if not (continuation of a
       dependent question that started with הֲ) [11.a]
    b. surely (negative, with negative) [asseverative]
       [11.b]
    c. but [adversative] [11.c]
    d. unless [exceptive] [11.d]
12. וְלֹא and if not, (then) [conditional-negative] [12]
13. without, un-, -less (negates a noun or adjective into
    the opposite) [13]
14. nothing (substantive) [14]
15. (collocations) [15]
    a. (בְּלֹא) [15.a]
    b. (כְּלֹא) [15.b]
    c. (הֲלֹא) [15.c]
    d. (שֶׁלֹא and טֶרֶם לֹא) [15.d]

Arnold & Choi – adversative clause, pp. 194–95 (§5.2.10); oath
    sentence, pp. 201–2 (§5.3.2); negative sentence, p. 204 (§5.3.5)
BDB – in predication; not in predication; as a substantive;
    with prefixes, pp. 518–20
DCH – factual statement of negative character; consequence
    or cause; adversative (followed by perfect); questions;
    conditional (in protasis or apodosis); with infinitive
    absolute and perfect; factual or descriptive statement or
    assurance; consequence or purpose; adversative (followed
    by imperfect); prohibition, instruction, or plea (followed
    by imperfect); prohibition (אֲשֶׁר לֹא); refusal or denial;
    in questions usually preceded by interrogative particle;
    with infinitive absolute and imperfect; followed by par-
    ticiple; with infinitive; followed by nominal clause; not
    followed by verb or nominal clause (noun or preposition);
    substantivized relative particle; [substantive]; interjection;

הֲלֹא or וְלֹא modifying an entire clause or sentence; miscellaneous collocations, pp. 4:485–95

Gesenius – negative sentence, pp. 478–83 (§152)

Joüon & Muraoka – negative clause, pp. 567–73 (§160a–e, o, oa); clause of curse and oath, pp. 582–84 (§165)

Van der Merwe – negation of a statement; negation of a directive; negation in oaths; negation and כָּל; negation of a marked relative clause; negation of a zero relative clause; constituent negative, pp. 463–66 (§41.9)

Waltke & O'Connor – negative adverb, pp. 660–61 (§39.3.3); oath and wish exclamation, pp. 678–79 (§40.2.2)

Williams – objective denial of a fact; prohibition; to negate a gerundive infinitive; elliptic; to negate a predicate that is not a verb; privative, pp. 143–44 (§§395–400)

לְבַד (161x)

see I בַּד in *HALOT*, p. 109; *Holladay*, p. 33

ADVERB

1. alone, on one's own [singularity] [2.a]
2. לְבַד מִן except, apart from, beside [separation] [2.b]

BDB – separation; singularity; limitation; followed by מִן it becomes a preposition (מִלְּבַד), p. 94

DCH – [singularity]; [separation]; [followed by various prepositions or combined with מִן], pp. 4:509–11

Gesenius – substantive that becomes an adverb by the addition of לְ prefix, pp. 377–78 (§119c)

Hardy – part or portion; singularity; separation, pp. 152–54 (§4.10.2)

Joüon & Muraoka – adverbial accusative, pp. 304–5 (§102d)

Van der Merwe – indicates the singularity of entity; separation from a collection x, pp. 438–39 (§40.32)

לְבְלִי (3x; Isa 5:14; Job 38:41; 41:25)

see בְּלִי in *HALOT*, p. 133; *Holladay*, p. 41

ADVERB
1. without (with substantive) [5]

BDB – [privative], p. 115
DCH – [privative], p. 2:177

לָהֵן (2x; both in Ruth 1:13)

HALOT, p. 521; *Holladay*, p. 173

CONJUNCTION
1. therefore [inference]

BDB – inference, p. 529
DCH – inference, p. 4:521

לוּ (17x)/לֻא (2x; 2 Sam 18:12; 19:7)/לוּא (3x; 1 Sam 14:30; Isa 48:18; 63:19)

HALOT, p. 521; *Holladay*, p. 174

CONJUNCTION
1. oh that . . . might, if only . . . might, let . . . (with imperfect as prayer, devout wish, not jussive) [1]
   • maybe, now if, what if, suppose . . .
2. please (with imperative) [2]
3. would that, if only (with perfect: past contrary to fact) [3]
4. if only (with participle, with יֵשׁ, and in nominal clause) [4]
5. certainly, good (asseverative) [5]

Arnold & Choi – unreal conditional clause, p. 187 (§5.2.2b)

BDB – stating a case which has not been, or is not likely to be realized; [wish], p. 530

DCH – introducing irreal condition; supposition; exclamation, pp. 4:521–22

Gesenius – desiderative sentence, p. 477 (§151e); conditional sentence, pp. 494–95 (§159l–n)

Joüon & Muraoka – optative clause, p. 579 (§163c); conditional clause, pp. 592–93 (§167f, k)

Van der Merwe – introduces hypothetical condition, expressing a wish, pp. 439–40 (§40.33)

Waltke & O'Connor – conditional clause, pp. 637–38 (§38.2e); oath and wish exclamation, p. 680 (§40.2.2d)

Williams – unreal condition; optative, p. 162 (§§459a, 460)

לוּלֵי/לוּלֵא (14x)

HALOT, p. 524; *Holladay*, p. 174

NEGATIVE PARTICLE
   1. if not, unless (contrary to fact) [conditional] [1]
   2. surely (affirmative) [2]

Arnold & Choi – unreal conditional clause, p. 187 (§5.2.2b)

BDB – [negative unreal condition], [exceptive], p. 530

DCH – unreal conditional particle; emphatic adverb; [exceptive], p. 4:530

Gesenius – conditional sentence, p. 497 (§159x)

Joüon & Muraoka – conditional clause, pp. 592–93 (§167f, k)

Van der Merwe – introduces a hypothetical condition, pp. 466–67 (§41.10)

Waltke & O'Connor – conditional clause, pp. 637–38 (§38.2e)

Williams – negative unreal condition, pp. 162, 183–84 (§§459b, 516b)

לָכֵן (200x)

HALOT, p. 530; *Holladay*, p. 177

ADVERB
  1. therefore, because (before a threat or punishment) [1]
  2. in return for, for this [exchange] [2]
  3. assuredly, indeed, all right [asseverative] [3]

Arnold & Choi – response to a statement of conditions, p. 148 (§4.2.10b)

BDB – declaration or command after statement of grounds; statement of grounds in reply to an objection; inferring cause from the effect, pp. 486–87

DCH – introducing a following fact, idea, etc.; [asseverative], pp. 4:547–48

Joüon & Muraoka – causal and explicative clause, p. 601 (§170o)

Van der Merwe – grounds; consequence; to acknowledge the validity of an assertion in argumentative dialogues; explanatory, pp. 440–43 (§40.35)

Waltke & O'Connor – introduces a proposed or anticipated response after a statement of certain conditions, p. 666 (§39.3.4.e)

לָמָה/לָמֶה/לָמָה/לָמָה (178x)

see מָה in *HALOT*, pp. 551–52; *Holladay*, p. 184

PREPOSITION
  1. to what end? [develops into] why? [interrogative] [D.3.a]
    • (accusingly)
    • (defensively)
    • לָמָה זֶּה why not?
    • לָמָה לִּי what is it to me?

CONJUNCTION

1. so that . . . not, lest [negative result] [D.3.b]

BDB – [interrogative]: in expostulations; with an imperfect, often deprecating, or introducing rhetorically, the reason why something should, or should not, be done, p. 554

DCH – [interrogative]; [negative purpose], p. 5:160

Gesenius – introduces questions, which really contain an affirmation and are used to state the reason for a request or warning, p. 474 (§150e)

Joüon & Muraoka – specific questions, p. 576 (§161h)

Van der Merwe – question word, p. 348 (§39.11); interrogative: inquires as to the reason for a state of affairs or an action, p. 480 (§42.3.7)

Waltke & O'Connor – interrogative; used in a quasi-rhetorical way, introducing an undesirable alternative, p. 324 (§18.3c)

לְמַעַן (272x)

see מַעַן in *HALOT*, p. 614; *Holladay*, p. 207

PREPOSITION

1. with reference to, on account of, for the sake of, because of [causal] [1]

CONJUNCTION

1. (conjunction) [2]
   a. in order to (with infinitive) [purpose] [2.a]
   b. so that (with imperfect) [result] [2.b]
   c. (often the result is expressed as intent) [2.c]
      • (often with irony)

Arnold & Choi – purpose; causal, p. 128 (§4.1.11); final clause, pp. 187–88 (§5.2.3)

BDB – *preposition*: [causal]; [reason]; [purpose: followed by infinitive]; *conjunction*: [purpose: followed by imperfect], p. 775

DCH – *preposition*: [causal]; *conjunction*: [purpose], pp. 4:552–54

Gesenius – complex preposition as adverbial, p. 377 (§119c); final clause, p. 504 (§165b)

Hardy – purpose/result; cause, pp. 159–61 (§4.12.2.1–2)

Joüon & Muraoka – final clause, p. 596 (§168d); consecutive clause, p. 598 (§169g)

Van der Merwe – purpose (positive & negative); result; reason, pp. 443–47 (§40.36)

Waltke & O'Connor – complex preposition as noun, p. 221 (§11.3.1); telic particle, p. 511 (§31.6.1c); final and result clauses, pp. 638–40 (§38.3)

Williams – advantage; causal; purpose; result, pp. 134–35 (§§364–368)

לְנֶגֶד (32x)

see נֶגֶד in *HALOT*, p. 666; *Holladay*, p. 226

ADVERB

1. from . . . to, in front of (motion) [3.a]
2. opposite, in front of, before [positional] [3.b]
3. לְנֶגְדִּי against my (will) [hostile] [3.c]
4. לְנֶגְדִּי present with me, present to my mind [positive-moral] [3.d]
5. before (them) . . . there [negative-moral] [3.e]
6. לְנֶגְדָּם thence, straight forward, straight ahead [directional] [3.f]
7. with regard to [authority] [3.g]

BDB – [spatial]; figurative of what is visible morally, p. 617

DCH – [spatial]; [hostile]; [comparative]; [authority], pp. 5:603–4

לִפְנֵי (1103x)

see פָּנֶה in *HALOT*, pp. 941–42; *Holladay*, p. 294

PREPOSITION

1. before (with or without motion) (spatial) [D.4.a]
2. one in front of another [spatial] [D.4.b]
3. before (in front of someone in power) [D.4.c]
4. before (temporal) [D.4.d]
5. according to the opinion of, in the view of [estimative] [D.4.e]
6. at the disposal of, for [D.4.f]
7. in the manner of, as if it were [D.4.g]

Arnold & Choi – locative; temporal; perceptual, pp. 128–29 (§4.1.12); succeeding temporal action, p. 190 (§5.2.4b)

BDB – [supervision/perception/estimation]; other phrases; position; places; temporal; [comparative], pp. 816–17

DCH – [spatial]; [temporal], pp. 4:557–63

Gesenius – substantive in construct regarded as in the genitive, p. 297 (§101b)

Hardy – locative; temporal, pp. 169–73 (§4.15.2)

Joüon & Muraoka – temporal clause, p. 588 (§166k)

Van der Merwe – frontal location; anterior temporal location, pp. 357–60 (§39.13)

Waltke & O'Connor – complex preposition as noun, p. 221 (§11.3.1)

Williams – locative; temporal; viewpoint; comparison, pp. 135–36 (§§369–373)

לִפְנִים (23x)

see פָּנֶה in *HALOT*, p. 940; *Holladay*, pp. 293–94

ADVERB

1. earlier, earliest, formerly, previously, in times past
   (temporal) [B.2]
   • מִלְּפָנִים beforehand, from the beginning = at all
   times

BDB – locative; temporal, p. 816
DCH – [temporal]; [locative], pp. 4:563–64
Hardy – locative; temporal, p. 169
Joüon & Muraoka – temporal: anteriority, pp. 587–88 (§166k)
Van der Merwe – unspecified period of time, anterior to the
   point of speaking, p. 360 (§39.13.2)
Waltke & O'Connor – allative adverbial, p. 205 (§11.2.10b)

מְאֹד (300x)

HALOT, p. 538; *Holladay*, p. 180

ADVERB
1. strength, power (substantive) [1]
2. very, in the highest degree [2]
   • (prepositive)
   • (separated)
   • מְאֹד מְאֹד very greatly, very much indeed
     (intensifying/reinforcing)

Arnold & Choi – intensive, pp. 149–50 (§4.2.12)
BDB – [substantive]; adverbial accusative [of degree], p. 547
DCH – adverb [of degree]; adjective; [substantive], pp. 5:103–7
Gesenius – adverbial accusative [of degree], p. 294 (§100c)
Joüon & Muraoka – absolute superlative or elative, p. 491
   (§141k)
Van der Merwe – superlative degree, p. 271 (§30.4.2.1c);
   adverb of degree, p. 380 (§40.1.3.1c)
Waltke & O'Connor – absolute superlative p. 268 (§14.5b);

adverb of degree, p. 659 (§39.3.1i); intensifying adverb, p. 668 (39.3.4g)

מִן־אָז/מֵאָז (19x)

see אָז in *HALOT*, p. 26; *Holladay*, p. 8

ADVERB
   1. formerly, before, before now, earlier [temporal] [4.a]

PREPOSITION
   1. since [temporal] [4.b]

CONJUNCTION
   1. since [temporal] [4.c]

BDB – *adverb*: temporal; *preposition* or *conjunction*: temporal, p. 32
DCH – *adverb*: [temporal]; *preposition*: [temporal]; *conjunction*: [temporal], p. 1:220
Gesenius – temporal clause, p. 502 (§164.d)
Joüon & Muraoka – *preposition*: temporal, p. 460 (§133e)
Van der Merwe – *adverb*: duration of time in the distant past, pp. 386–87 (§40.6)
Waltke & O'Connor – temporal clause, pp. 643–44 (§38.7)

מֵאַיִן (17x)

see II אַיִן in *HALOT*, p. 42; *Holladay*, p. 13

INTERROGATIVE ADVERB
   1. from where? [question]
   2. from where (indirect question)

3. whence (rhetorical question)

BDB – [interrogative], p. 32
DCH – interrogative, p. 1:220
Joüon & Muraoka – interrogative adverb, p. 306 (§102i)
Waltke & O'Connor – locative in reference, interrogative
    in use, p. 327 (§18.4)

מֵאֵת/מֵאִתּוֹ, etc. (170x)

see II אֵת in *HALOT*, p. 101; *Holladay*, p. 31

PREPOSITION

    1. out of, from (after verbs of removing) [separative]
       [4]
- through [instrumental]
- bought from (acquisition)
- due from [rights or dues]
- by my orders [authority]

BDB – [acquisition]; rights or dues; origination; place,
    pp. 86–87
DCH – [source/separation/figurative], pp. 1:452–53
Gesenius – combination of prepositions (each retaining its
    full force), p. 378 (§199d)
Joüon & Muraoka – compound preposition, p. 462 (§133j)

מִבְּלִי (25x)

see בְּלִי in *HALOT*, p. 133; *Holladay*, pp. 40–41

ADVERB

    1. without [privative] [4]

BDB – causal; מִן expressing negation, and בְּלִי being pleonastic; partitive, pp. 115–16

DCH – [*substantive*]; [*privative*], pp. 2:177–78

Gesenius – two negatives in the same sentence make the negation more emphatic, p. 483 (§152y)

Joüon & Muraoka – negative is pleonastic after מִן in a privative or negative sense, p. 573 (§160p)

מַדּוּעַ (71x)/מַדְּעַ (1x; Ezek 18:19)

HALOT, p. 548; *Holladay*, p. 183

INTERROGATIVE ADVERB
1. on what account?, why?

BDB – adverb: [interrogative], p. 396

DCH – interrogative adverb, pp. 5:145–46

Gesenius – interrogative sentences, p. 476 (§150m)

Joüon & Muraoka – interrogative adverb, p. 306 (§102i)

Waltke & O'Connor – used for question-word questions, p. 684 (§40.3a)

מָה (572x)

HALOT, pp. 550–52; *Holladay*, pp. 183–84

INTERROGATIVE PRONOUN
1. what? how? (interrogative pronoun) [A.1]
   • (bewildered, reproachful interrogative)
2. (indirect question) [A.2]
3. what?, why then?, what kind of? (with זֶה) [A.3]
4. what? (elliptical) [A.4]
   • (with כִּי; without כִּי; with לְ infinitive, with participle; with אֶת; with שֶׁ)

5. what = that which (after verb of enquiry/telling, examination/seeing, inspection or communication, etc.) [A.5]
6. מָה . . . לֹא does not know about what = anything, nothing at all (negative expressions) [A.6]
7. (that) which, whatever (with שֶׁ) (correlative) [A.7]
8. whatever, anything (indefinite pronoun) [A.8]

INTERROGATIVE ADVERB

1. how! how much! what! [exclamatory] [B]
   - (ironically)
   - (plaintively)
   - how is it that . . . ? why? [interrogative]
2. how could I . . . ? = I have not; what have we . . . ? = we have nothing (negation) [C]
3. (with prepositions) [D]
   a. בַּמֶּה or בַּמָּה with what?, by what means?, wherein?, wherefore?, why?, how?; [interrogative] [D.1]
   b. כַּמֶּה or כַּמָּה how much?, how many?; [interrogative of quantity] [D.2]
   c. לָמָה or לָמֶה or לְמָה or לְמָה [D.3]
      - to what end? [develops into] why? [interrogative] [D.3.a]
      - so that . . . not, lest (conjunction) [negative result] [D.3.b]
   d. עַד־מֶה or עַד־מָה how long now? [temporal-interrogative] [D.4]
   e. עַל(־)מֶה and עַל(־)מָה on what account? [causal-interrogative] [D.5]

Arnold & Choi – interrogative sentence, p. 200 (§5.3.1c)
BDB – *interrogative pronoun*: direct questions; indirect questions; insinuation of blame, or reproach, or contempt; rhetorical negative; [independent relative]; *adverb*:

interrogative; exclamatory; *indefinite pronoun*; with prepositions, pp. 552–54

DCH – interrogative; exclamation; as combined existential and interrogative particle; as combined interrogative and conditional particle; ail or need; [quantity]; indefinite pronoun; as combined relative particle and antecedent; independent relative with שֶׁ or אֲשֶׁר; with various other words, pp. 5:150–62

Gesenius – interrogative pronoun, pp. 443–44 (§137c); predicate of a noun-clause, pp. 451–52 (§141b); exclamation, p. 471 (§148a–b)

Joüon & Muraoka – interrogative pronoun, pp. 105–7, 501–3 (§§37, 144); indirect question, pp. 575–76 (§161g); exclamatory clause, p. 578 (§162a)

Van der Merwe – complementizer in indefinite expressions, pp. 310–11 (§36.5.2); inquires about the nature of a thing or event; inquires about the reason for a state of affairs or event; introduces a rhetorical question; exclamatory; indefinite pronoun, pp. 478–80 (§42.3.6, 7)

Waltke & O'Connor – inanimate pronoun, pp. 317–18, 322–27 (§18.1e, 3)

Williams – interrogative pronoun; indefinite pronoun; interrogative adverb; exclamation; in rhetorical questions that expect a negative answer, pp. 52–53 (§§124–128)

מְהֵרָה (20x)

HALOT, p. 554; *Holladay*, p. 185

ADVERB
1. haste, speed, hurry [substantive] [1]
2. hurriedly, quickly, in a hurry [manner] [2]

BDB – [substantive]; adverb, p. 555

DCH – [*substantive*]; *adverb*, p. 5:167

Joüon & Muraoka – adverbial accusative, pp. 304–5
(§102d)

Waltke & O'Connor – manner adverb, p. 659 (§39.3.1j)

מָחָר (52x)

HALOT, pp. 571–72; *Holladay*, p. 191

ADVERB

    1. next day, tomorrow (adverbial accusative) [1]
    2. in the future, in time to come [2]

BDB – [*substantive*]; *adverbial accusative* [of time],
    pp. 563–64
DCH – [*substantive*]; *adverb* [of time], p. 5:229
Gesenius – adverbial accusative, p. 294 (§100c)
Waltke & O'Connor – temporal adverb, p. 659 (§39.3.1h)

מָחֳרָת (32x)

HALOT, p. 572; *Holladay*, p. 191

ADVERB

    1. the following day (substantive) [1]
    2. (on) the next day [temporal] [2]
        a. (adverbial accusative) [2.a]
        b. מִמָּחֳרָת on the following day [2.b]
          • מִמָּחֳרָת on the day after

BDB – [*substantive*]; [*adverb*], p. 564
DCH – [*substantive*]; *adverb*: [temporal], p. 5:230
Waltke & O'Connor – temporal adverb, p. 658
    (§39.3.1h)

מַטָּה (19x)

HALOT, p. 573; *Holladay*, p. 192

ADVERB
1. below, beneath (locative) [1]
   - מַטָּה מַטָּה with יָרַד deeper and deeper, lower and lower
2. לְמַטָּה downward [directional] [2]
   - לְמַטָּה מֵעָוֹן less than deserved [figurative]
3. מִלְמַטָּה below (on), beneath (on) [3]

BDB – [directional], p. 641
DCH – [directional], pp. 5:234–35
Waltke & O'Connor – adverb of location, p. 658 (§39.3.1g)

מִטֶּרֶם (1x; Hag 2:15)

see טֶרֶם in *HALOT*, p. 380; *Holladay*, p. 125

PREPOSITION
1. even before (with infinitive) [temporal] [3.a]

BDB – [temporal], p. 382
DCH – [temporal], p. 3:376
Gesenius – adverbial combination of substantive with preposition, p. 306 (§104a)
Van der Merwe – refers to a point in time prior to that of the referent of the construction in its scope, irrespective of the time frame involved, pp. 462–63 (§41.8)

מִי (423x)

HALOT, p. 575; *Holladay*, p. 192

INTERROGATIVE

1. who? [interrogative] [1]
2. מִי בְכָל who (of all)?, what (one is there of)? (partitive) [2]
3. (with a dependent clause) [3]
4. (indirect question) [4]
5. (with imperfect) [5]
   a. מִי יֹאמַר who may say [5.a]
   b. (as an unreal/unattainable wish) [5.b]
      • (מִי יִתֵּן as an optative particle)
      • מִי יִתֵּן יָדַעְתִּי I wished I had known
6. whoever (indefinite pronoun) [6]
7. (interjection) [7]
   a. as who [develops into] how! (= מָה) [7.a]
   b. where? [7.b]
8. (miscellaneous) [8]
   • מִי הוּא
   • מִי זֶה/זֹאת
   • מִי in negative sense

Arnold & Choi – interrogative sentence, p. 200 (§5.3.1c); wish sentence, p. 202 (§5.3.3b)

BDB – interrogative of persons; in the genitive; in an indirect question; [partitive]; strengthened and emphatic forms of interrogative; various rhetorical uses; [indefinite pronoun]; following a verb (only once: 2 Sam 18:12), pp. 566–67

DCH – interrogative; relative pronoun; colloquial; [indefinite pronoun], pp. 5:242–50

Gesenius – interrogative pronoun, pp. 443–44 (§137); predicate of a noun-clause, pp. 451–52 (§141b); exclamation, p. 471 (§148c)

Joüon & Muraoka – interrogative pronoun, pp. 105, 501–3 (§§37a; 144); indirect question, pp. 575–76 (§161g); optative clause, pp. 579–80 (§163d)

Van der Merwe – complementizer in indefinite expressions, pp. 310–11 (§36.5.2); inquires about the identity of a person or a group of people; introduces a rhetorical question; expresses a wish; indefinite pronoun, pp. 480–82 (§42.3.8)

Waltke & O'Connor – eliciting the identification or classifications of persons in questions; indirect question ("relative use"); indefinite; exclamatory question; rhetorical question; wish; doubt, pp. 318–22 (§18.2)

Williams – interrogative pronoun; indefinite pronoun; optative; interrogative adverb, pp. 51–52 (§§119–123)

מִלְּפְנֵי (75x)

see פָּנֶה in *HALOT*, p. 942; *Holladay*, p. 294

PREPOSITION

1. away from [spatial] [D.4.h]
   - on account of, because of [causal]

BDB – spatial position; source or cause; temporal, pp. 817–18
DCH – place; time; [causal], pp. 4:562–63
Van der Merwe – *x* moves from the presence of *y*, p. 365 (§39.15)
Waltke & O'Connor – locative; causal, p. 221 (§11.3.1a)

מִן (7,540x)

HALOT, pp. 597–99; *Holladay*, pp. 200–201

PREPOSITION

1. out of, away from (locative/spatial) [1]
   a. out of (beginning-point of motion) [1.a]
      - from (the door-hole) = through
   b. (direction of movement with אֶל) [1.b]

   c. where something is (the place in whose direction
     something is) [1.c]
2. (temporal) [2]
   a. since, from (the time of) [2.a]
   b. immediately after, just after [2.b]
   c. after [2.c]
   d. (from the time when something happens) [2.d]
3. [source] [3]
   a. of (material form which something is made) [3.a]
   b. from (place of origin) [3.b]
4. (designates) [4]
   a. from, with, by (causal) [4.a]
   b. issued by (originator) [4.b]
   c. by, from (logical subject of a passive verb) [4.c]
5. (position or standard of an assessor) [5]
   a. I am small, unimportant for (= I am too small for,
     I am unworthy of) [5.a]
   b. more than (comparative) [5.b]
6. in consequence of, because of (causal) [6]
7. (with verbs of fearing, hiding, protecting, warning,
   guarding) [7]
   a. from, against [7.a]
   b. far from [develops into] without [privative] [7.b]
8. (partitive) [8]
   a. from the whole of, one of, from among (part of
     the whole) [8.a]
   b. (after adjective) (superlative) [8.b]
   c. one of, some of (proportion of the part to the
     whole is not specified) [8.c]
      • not one of, none of (negated)
   d. some of, any of (undetermined part of the whole)
     [8.d]
9. (מִן with infinitive) [9]
   a. because [causal] [9.a]

   b. so that not [negative result] [9.b]
   c. after (temporal) [9.c]
10. (with other prepositions) [10]
   a. (preceding the preposition) [10.a]
   b. (following the preposition) [10.b]

CONJUNCTION
   1. lest, so that . . . not [negative result] [11]

Arnold & Choi – source; temporal; material; causal; estimative; partitive; privative; comparative; compound, pp. 129–31 (§4.1.13); causal clause, p. 192 (§5.2.5b)

BDB – with verbs expressing separation or removal; [source]; [cause]; partitive; temporal; [with various prepositions: geographical, metaphorical, temporal, variation/interval]; comparative; prefixed to an infinitive; as conjunction before a finite verb (only once: Deut 33:11); [substantive], in association with various other prepositions; in compound, followed by other preposition, particle or adverb, pp. 1100–1101

DCH – direction; temporal; material; partitive; comparative; privative; locative; causal; agency; instrumental; estimative; hostility or protection; compounds; pp. 5:337–45

Gesenius – distance; separation; source; partitive; in final or consecutive clauses, pp. 382–83 (§119v – z); comparative; removal or severance, pp. 429–30 (§133a–e)

Joüon & Muraoka – separation and distance; material; cause; source or origin; partitive; explanation; temporal; comparison; causal; consecutive, p. 460 (§133e); causal and explicative clause, p. 600 (§170i)

Van der Merwe – spatial detachment; origin; location/source (of an activity or attitude); partitive; temporal detachment; spatial location; temporal orientation; comparison; privative; instrument; ground, pp. 360–64 (§39.14)

Waltke & O'Connor – spatial; temporal; ablative; locational; material; author or authority from whom a standard or truth originated; cause; means; agency; partitive; privative; comparative, pp. 212–14 (§11.2.11); comparative degree, pp. 263–67 (§14.4); distributive expressions, pp. 288–89 (§15.6)

Williams – separative; starting time; comparative; absolute comparative; causal; means; agent; privative; source; relationship in space; time; standpoint; partitive; emphatic; explicative; inclusive, pp. 120–25 (§§315–327)

מִנֶּגֶד (26x)

see נֶגֶד in *HALOT*, p. 667; *Holladay*, p. 226

ADVERB
1. on the other side, opposite [spatial] [4.a]
2. apart, aloof, aside [spatial] [4.b]

PREPOSITION
1. away from [ablative] [5.a]
2. far from [separative] [5.b]
3. before, in front of, abreast (Neh 3:25, a correction by *Holladay* of *HALOT*'s Neh 3:5) [positional] [5.c]
4. (מִנֶּגֶד לְ) [5.d]

BDB – *adverb*: [spatial]; *preposition*: [separative]; [positional], p. 617

DCH – *preposition*: [spatial/separative]; *adverb*: [positional], p. 5:604

מֵסַב (4x)

HALOT, p. 604; *Holladay*, p. 203

ADVERB

1. [substantive] [1]
   a. round table, banquet, circle of feasters [1.a]
   b. neighborhood, surroundings (plural) [1.b]
2. round about, all around me [locative] (plural suffix) [2]

BDB – [substantive]; adverb: [locative], p. 687
DCH – [substantive]; adverb: [locative], p. 5:359
Waltke & O'Connor – adverb of location, p. 658 (§39.3.1g)

מְסִבָּה (1x; Job 37:12)

HALOT, p. 604; Holladay, p. 203

ADVERB

1. round about [manner] [1]

BDB – adverb, p. 687
DCH – [substantive], p. 3:359

מִסָּבִיב (44x)

see סָבִיב in HALOT, p. 740; Holladay, p. 252

ADVERB

1. on every side, around and about [spatial proximity]
   [A.3]

BDB – [spatial proximity], p. 687
DCH – directional; partitive; privative, p. 6:110

מָסָח (1x; 2 Kgs 11:6)

HALOT, p. 605; Holladay, p. 203

ADVERB
   1. alternating

BDB – dubious word, probably textual error, p. 587
DCH – adverb, pp. 5:361–62

מְעַט (101x)

HALOT, p. 611; *Holladay*, p. 206

ADVERB
   1. (substantive) [1]
   2. (with genitive) [2]
   3. (postpositional) [3]
       a. (as *nomen rectum*) [3.a]
       b. (appositional) [3.b]
   4. (adjective) [4]
   5. (adverb) [5]
       a. in a small amount, a little [5.a]
          • עוֹד מְעַט a little more, nearly
       b. for a short time, עוֹד מְעַט soon, מְעַט מְעַט
          gradually, by and by (temporal) [5.b]
   6. (with prepositions) [6]
       a. כִּמְעַט nearly, pleonastic following לוּלֵי [6.a]
          • easily, quickly, soon, a short moment, scarcely
   7. too little (elative) [7]

BDB – *substantive*; *adverb*: accusative of place, of time,
   of degree, repeated = gradually, pp. 589–90
DCH – [*substantive*]; *adverb* [of degree], pp. 5:393–96
Joüon & Muraoka – elliptical comparison, p. 490 (§141i)
Van der Merwe – degree, p. 380 (§40.1.3.1c)
Waltke & O'Connor – adverb of degree, p. 659 (§39.3.1i);
   emphatic adverb, p. 662 (§39.3.4b)

מֵעַל (140x)

see II מַעַל in *HALOT*, p. 613; *Holladay*, pp. 206–7

ADVERB

1. above [spatial] [1]
   a. בַּשָּׁמַיִם מִמַּעַל [1.a]
   b. מִמַּעַל לְ above someone, something [1.b]
      • on top of = מִמַּעַל עַל
2. מָ/מַעְלָה upwards, above (locative) [2]
   a. מַעְלָה מָעְלָה higher and higher, וָמַעְלָה and
      further [2.a]
      • מִן־הַיּוֹם הַהוּא וָמָעְלָה from that day onward
        (temporal)
   b. לְמַעְלָה (to) above [2.b]
      • עַד־לְמַעְלָה (illness) was quite severe [figurative]
      • לְמַעְלָה מִן beyond, over and above,
        מִן ... וּלְמַעְלָה from there upwards
   c. מִלְמַעְלָה/מְעְלָה down from above, above [2.c]
      • עַל ... מִלְמַעְלָה on top of, above, upon (them)

BDB – *substantive*; *adverb*: [spatial]; with locative ה,
   pp. 751–52
DCH – [*substantive*]; *adverb*: [spatial], pp. 5:402–4
Waltke & O'Connor – adverb of location, p. 658 (§39.3.1g)

מֵעַל (303x)

see II עַל in *HALOT*, p. 827; *Holladay*, p. 273

PREPOSITION

1. downwards from, above and outside [8.a]
2. over, on [8.b]
3. beside, by [8.c]
4. more than (comparative) [8.d]

BDB – idiomatically, when removal, motion, etc., from a
surface is involved; of relief from a burden or trouble;
[spatial], pp. 758–59

DCH – [spatial]; [experiential]; [hostility]; excess;
comparison; pre-eminence, exaltation, pp. 6:396–98

Gesenius – adverb of place, pp. 377–78 (§119c)

Joüon & Muraoka – marks relief from harassment, p. 461
(§133f)

Waltke & O'Connor – adverb of place, p. 221 (11.3.2a)

מֵעַל־פְּנֵי (27x)

see פָּנֶה in *HALOT*, p. 944; *Holladay*, p. 294

PREPOSITION
1. away from, really off the surface [spatial/
metaphorical] [D.9]

BDB – [spatial/metaphorical], p. 819
DCH – [spatial/metaphorical], p. 6:721

מֵעִם (71x)

see עַם in *HALOT*, p. 840; *Holladay*, p. 275

PREPOSITION
1. from having a connection with (meaning forward
from, from ... to) [4.a]
2. more than (comparative) [4.b]

BDB – [spatial]; possession or custody; origination or
authorship, pp. 768–69

DCH – motion, removal; dealings with; agency; origin;
request, requirement; comparison; cause, p. 6:462

Gesenius – combination of prepositions (each retaining its full force), p. 378 (§119d)

Joüon & Muraoka – compound preposition, p. 462 (§133j)

מֵעַתָּה (13x)

see עַתָּה in *HALOT*, p. 902; *Holladay*, p. 287

ADVERB

1. from now on [temporal] [5]
   - (מֵעַתָּה וְעַד־עוֹלָם)

BDB – [temporal], p. 774
DCH – [temporal], p. 6:634
Van der Merwe – temporal adverb, p. 452 (§40.39)

מִפְּנֵי (307x)

see פָּנֶה in *HALOT*, p. 943; *Holladay*, p. 294

PREPOSITION

1. away from a position, from in front [spatial] [D.5.a]
2. to go away from [ablative] [D.5.b]
3. in front of, in the face of, before [positional] [D.5.c]
4. on account of, because (causal) [D.5.d]

Arnold & Choi – ablative; spatial; causal, p. 132 (§4.1.14)
BDB – [spatial]; often with suggestion of causation; implying causation more distinctly; of the cause, whether nearer or more remote, p. 818
DCH – [spatial]; [causal]; [ablative], pp. 6:716–19
Hardy – composite locative; cause, pp. 184–85 (4.18.2)
Joüon & Muraoka – causal, p. 600 (§170i)

Van der Merwe – detachment (movement & attitude); ground, pp. 365–66 (§39.15)

Waltke & O'Connor – locative; causal, p. 221 (§11.3.1a)

Williams – locative; causal, pp. 136–37 (§§374–376)

מַר (2x; Isa 33:7; Ezek 27:30)

see I מַר in *HALOT*, p. 629; *Holladay*, p. 213

ADVERB

1. bitterly [manner] [2.b]

BDB – adjective; substantive; adverb [of manner], p. 600

DCH – adjective; adverb [of manner]; [substantive], p. 5:472

Joüon & Muraoka – [manner], p. 304 (§102c)

נָא (404x)

see I נָא in *HALOT*, pp. 656–57; *Holladay*, p. 223

ENCLITIC PARTICLE OF EMPHASIS/URGENCY

1. surely, please, do, just (with imperative) [1]

2. (with emphatic imperative) [2]

3. (with cohortative) [3]

4. (with jussive) [4]

5. (following a suffix) [5]

6. (following a particle) [6]
  a. הִנֵּה־נָא now look [6.a]
  b. let there not be (אַל־נָא with imperfect/jussive) [6.b]
  c. if I may, if I have (with אִם) [6.c]
  d. אוֹי־נָא oh dear! [6.d]
  e. אַיֵּה־נָא so where? [6.e]
  f. (in special phrases/misc.) [6.f]

BDB – entreaty or admonition; precative; prayer or desire; joined to conjunctions and interjections, pp. 816–17

DCH – politeness; inferiors addressing superiors; emphasis; logical consequence, pp. 5:576–77

Gesenius – optative or precative in use of the cohortative and jussive, pp. 320–21 (§§108c, 109b); to soften down an imperative, p. 324 (§110d)

Joüon & Muraoka – entreating; attention, pp. 322–23, 346 (§§105c, d, 114b)

Van der Merwe – a polite request, pp. 171, 485 (§§19.5.2.2, 44.10)

Waltke & O'Connor – polite exclamations; inference, pp. 683–84 (§40.2.5c)

נֶגֶד (151x)

HALOT, pp. 666–67; *Holladay*, p. 226

PREPOSITION

1. that which is opposite, that which corresponds, opposite, counterpart (substantive) [1]
2. (preposition with genitive or suffix) [2]
    a. in front of, in the presence of, before [spatial proximity] [2.a]
    b. opposite to, over against [spatial opposition] [2.b]
    c. intention, judgement, opinion [mental opposition] [2.c]
    d. immediately in front, straight forward [spatial proximity] [2.d]
    e. corresponding [spatial correspondence] [2.e]
    f. contrary, against [hostile opposition] [2.f]
3. (לְנֶגֶד) [3]
    a. from ... to, in front of (motion) [3.a]
    b. opposite, in front of, before [positional] [3.b]
    c. לְנֶגְדִּי against my (will) [hostile] [3.c]

d. לְנֶגְדִּי present with me, present to my mind [positive-moral] [3.d]

e. before (them) . . . there [negative-moral] [3.e]

f. לְנֶגְדָּם thence, straight forward, straight ahead [directional] [3.f]

g. with regard to [authority] [3.g]

4. (מִנֶּגֶד, adverb) [4]

a. on the other side, opposite [spatial] [4.a]

b. apart, aloof, aside [spatial] [4.b]

5. (מִנֶּגֶד, preposition) [5]

a. straight away from [ablative] [5.a]

b. far from [separative] [5.b]

c. before, in front of [positional] [5.c]

d. opposite, over against [positional] [5.d]

6. עַד־נֶגֶד as far as/up to (a point) opposite [locative] [6]

a. נֶגְדָה־נָּא in the sight of [6.a]

BDB – *adverbial accusative*: locally, mentally; with prepositions, p. 617

DCH – [spatial]; [proximity]; [hostile opposition], pp. 5:603–4

Hardy – locative, pp. 95–97 (§3.8.3)

Van der Merwe – frontal opposition (spatial & mental); observable proximity (spatial & mental), pp. 366–67 (§39.16)

נֶגֶד פְּנֵי (5x)

see פָּנֶה in *HALOT*, p. 943; *Holladay*, p. 294

PREPOSITION

1. in the presence of, before [spatial] [D.6]

• wrong in your eyes, against your view (figurative)

• (evil/sinister purpose)

• מִנֶּגֶד פְּנֵי far from

נֹכַח (25x)

HALOT, pp. 698–99; *Holladay*, p. 238

PREPOSITION
1. what is/lies opposite (substantive) [1]
2. preposition [2]
   a. opposite [positional] [2.a]
   b. in front, place before oneself = consider agreeable (metaphorical) [2.b]
   c. (with prepositions) [2.c]
      - אֶל־נֹכַח toward the opposite direction
      - לְנֹכַח directly in front of; (to pray) on behalf; (adverbial) looking straight ahead
      - עַד־נֹכַח to a position opposite

BDB – [substantival]; *adverbial accusative*; combined with prepositions, p. 647

DCH – [substantival]; *preposition*: [positional]; נֹכַח לְ (positional); לְנֹכַח (positional or interest); *adverb*: [directional]; [with other prepositions], pp. 5:691–92

Hardy – *substantive*: location or direction; *preposition*: locative, p. 98 (§3.9.2)

Van der Merwe – spatial (direct frontal opposition), pp. 367–68 (§39.17)

נֹכַח פְּנֵי (6x)

see פָּנֶה in *HALOT*, p. 943; *Holladay*, p. 294

PREPOSITION
1. before the presence of [spatial/figurative] [D.7]

נֶצַח (4x)/נֵצַח (39x)

see I נֵצַח in *HALOT*, p. 716; *Holladay*, p. 244

ADVERB

1. splendour, luster, glory [substantive] [1]
2. duration [2]
   a. נֶצַח נְצָחִים throughout eternity [2.a]
   b. forever [2.b]
   c. with לְ, forever [2.c]
      • לָנֶצַח
      • עַד־נֶצַח
3. לָנֶצַח successful (legal) [3]

BDB – [substantive]; [adverb], p. 664
DCH – [substantive]; [adverb], pp. 5:739–40
Waltke & O'Connor – temporal adverb, p. 658 (§39.3.1h)

סָבִיב (336x)

HALOT, p. 740; Holladay, p. 252

ADVERB

1. surroundings, circuit (substantive) [A.1]
2. on all sides, all around [spatial proximity] [A.2]
   • סָבִיב סָבִיב all around
3. מִסָּבִיב on every side, around and about [spatial proximity] [A.3]
4. סָבִיב לְ around, (to) all around [spatial proximity] [A.4]

BDB – substantive; adverbial accusative: [spatial proximity];
   preposition: [spatial proximity]; with מִן, pp. 686–87
DCH – [substantive]; adverb: [spatial proximity]; סָבִיב
   repeated; spatial with מִן; preposition: [spatial proximity];
   [with various other prepositions], pp. 6:109–15
Hardy – substantive; adverb: locative; preposition: spatiodirectional, pp. 103–4 (§3.10.2)
Gesenius – circumference, p. 304 (§103o)

123

Joüon & Muraoka – adverbial accusative, pp. 304–5 (§102d); circumference (§102d)

Van der Merwe – a trajector *x* that encompasses a landmark *y*, pp. 368–69 (§39.18)

Waltke & O'Connor – locative, p. 657 (§39.3.1g)

עַד (1,258x)

see III עַד in *HALOT*, pp. 786–87; II עַד in *Holladay*, pp. 264–65

PREPOSITION

1. to, as far as (to) (locative/spatial) [A.1]
2. (temporal) [A.2]
   a. until, meanwhile [A.2.a]
   b. just before (meaning earlier) [A.2.b]
   c. during, as long as [A.2.c]
3. toward, on, to (mental disposition/direction of the mind, attention) [A.3]
4. to (measure or degree) [A.4]
5. up to (the degree of) = like, so . . . as (comparative) [A.5]
6. (with various other words) [A.6]
   a. (with numeral) [A.6.a]
   b. (with prepositions) [A.6.b]
   c. [develops into] (עַד־) [A.6.c]

CONJUNCTION

1. (with finite verb) [B.a]
2. (compound expressions) [B.b]
3. until the time (with לְ + infinitive) [B.c]

Arnold & Choi – locative; temporal; degree, pp. 132–33 (§4.1.15); temporal clause, p. 190 (§5.2.4b)

BDB – *preposition*: spatial; temporal; degree (also in comparisons); *conjunction*: [temporal]; degree, pp. 723–25

DCH – *preposition*: place; direction; time; degree or extent; range or class of objects; compound prepositions; *adverb*: [asseverative]; [concessive]; compound adverbs; *conjunction*: [temporal]; [concomitant circumstances]; compound conjunctions, pp. 6:251–67

Gesenius – progress; duration, p. 297 (§101a)

Joüon & Muraoka – with *yiqtol* for past action, p. 342 (§113k)

Van der Merwe – space; time; extension to an extreme dimension, pp. 369–71 (§39.19)

Waltke & O'Connor – spatial; temporal; durative; measure or degree; interest, pp. 215–16 (§11.2.12)

Williams – spatially terminative; locative; temporal; degree; inclusive; emphatic, pp. 118–20 (§§309–314)

עַד־מֶה/עַד־מָה (5x)

see מָה in *HALOT*, p. 552; *Holladay*, p. 184

PREPOSITION

1. how long now? [interrogative] [D.4]

BDB – [interrogative], p. 554

DCH – interrogative; *conjunction*: [temporal], p. 5:160

Gesenius – מָה with prepositions, p. 443 (§137b)

Van der Merwe – inquires about the *duration* of a state of affairs or events, p. 480 (§42.3.7.3)

נֶ֫גֶד(־)עַד (2x; Neh 3:16, 26)

see נֶ֫גֶד in *HALOT*, p. 667; *Holladay*, p. 226

ADVERB

1. as far as/up to (a point) opposite [locative] [6.a]
   • נֶגְדָּה־נָּא in the sight of

BDB – [locative], p. 617
DCH – [locative], p. 5:604

עַד־עַתָּה (9x)

see עַתָּה in *HALOT*, p. 902; *Holladay*, p. 287

ADVERB
  1. [temporal] [4]
     a. until now [4.a]
     b. until this time [4.b]

BDB – [temporal], p. 774
DCH – [temporal], p. 6:635
Van der Merwe – adverb that refers to a point in time concurrent with the speech time of an utterance, p. 452 (§40.39)

עֲדֶן (1x; Eccl 4:3)/עֲדֶנָה [*sic*: עֲדֶנָה] (1x; Eccl 4:2)

HALOT, p. 793; *Holladay*, p. 266

ADVERB
  1. so far, still, up to now, (not) yet [temporal]

BDB – [temporal], p. 725
DCH – [temporal], p. 6:282
Gesenius – [temporal], p. 295 (§100f)
Walkte & O'Connor – temporal adverb, p. 658 (§39.3.1h)

עוֹד (490x)

HALOT, pp. 795–96; *Holladay*, p. 267

ADVERB

1. (substantive) [1]
   a. duration, permanence, constancy, all the time = continually [1.a]
      • בְּעוֹד as long as
   b. remainder, rest [1.b]
2. still, always [continuance] [2]
   a. (in primary position) [2.a]
   b. (in secondary position) [2.b]
   c. first [2.c]
3. again, once more [repetition] [3]
4. still more, besides [4]
   • no one besides, no more

Arnold & Choi – manner, p. 150 (§4.2.13)

BDB – continuance; persistence; addition or repetition; with prefixes, pp. 728–29

DCH – continuance; addition; degree; repetition; with negation; [with various words], pp. 6:289–94

Gesenius – temporal clause, p. 501 (§164a)

Van der Merwe – repetition of an event; endurance of a state of affairs; extension of the number of a collection; extension of the quantity of a state; duration to be quantified; an unspecified long duration; addition, pp. 447–50 (§40.37)

Waltke & O'Connor – time extent, p. 657 (§39.3.1.d)

עֹלָם/עוֹלָם (437x)/עֵילוֹם (1x; 2 Chron 33:7)

HALOT, pp. 798–99; *Holladay*, pp. 267–68

ADVERB

1. long time, duration [substantive] [1]
2. (future time) [2]
   a. for all time, forever [2.a]

b. (with prepositions) [2.b]

c. עוֹלָמִים times to come [2.c]

3. a long time back [3]

4. (of God) [4]

5. (miscellaneous) [5]

BDB – [*substantive*]; [*adverb*], pp. 761–63

DCH – [*substantive*]; [*adverb*], pp. 6:300–307

Waltke & O'Connor – temporal adverb, p. 658 (§39.3.1h)

עַל (5,764x)

see II עַל in *HALOT*, pp. 825–27; *Holladay*, pp. 272–73

PREPOSITION

1. on, over, upon [spatial] [1]

a. on (also = in) [1.a]

- garment on someone

b. over, at, beside, above, up [spatial proximity] [1.b]

c. in front of, before (whenever one person stands and the other sits) [spatial proximity] [1.c]

- with יֵשׁ to be there for, or to stand by the side (of someone), support, help [metaphorical]

d. (duties and obligations which are incumbent on someone) [1.d]

- it is for me to, it is up to me, it is my duty (עָלַי with לְ and infinitive)
- (technical term in trade)

e. (physical or mental perceptions) [1.e]

- on, (meaning) relying on, supported by

f. above, (meaning) more than, greater than [comparative] [1.f]

g. on the side of, supported by [1.g]

2. on account of, because of, for the sake of [causal] [2]

על

3. with regard to, concerning [specification] [3]
4. according to, in the manner of, with regard, in the way of (manner) [4]
5. against [5]
   a. (in a hostile sense) [5.a]
   b. opposite, against, in spite of, despite, although [concessive] [5.b]
6. to, towards (motion) [6]
   a. (in the sense of אֶל) [6.a]
   b. in addition to [addition] [6.b, d]
   c. together with [accompaniment] [6.c]
7. from far off [spatiodirectional] [7]
8. (with מִן) [8]
   a. downwards from, above and outside [8.a]
   b. over, on [8.b]
   c. beside, by [8.c]
   d. more than (comparative) [8.d]

CONJUNCTION
1. (עַל as a conjunction) [9]
   a. because [causal] [9.a]
   b. עַל כִּי because [9.b]
      • עַל־אֲשֶׁר for the reason that, just because, on the ground that
   c. עַל לֹא notwithstanding, that . . . not [adversative] [9.c]
      • עַל אֲשֶׁר despite the fact that, in spite of
2. (in Psalm titles, according to a tune) [10]

Arnold & Choi – spatial/locative; duty; rank; causal; manner; adversative; accompaniment; interest; emotive, pp. 133–36 (§4.1.16); causal clause, p. 191 (§5.2.5); concessive clause, pp. 196–97 (§5.2.12)

BDB – *preposition*: substratum upon which an object rests or

129

an action is performed; excess, elevation or pre-eminence; addition; spatially suspended or extended; local and idiomatic contiguity or proximity; actual or figurative with verbs of motion; sometimes used with the force of a dative; with other particles; *conjunction*: [causal]; [adversative]; compounds, pp. 752–58

DCH – *preposition*: spatial; locations of feelings, perceptions, or states; direction of the mind or disposition; good fortune or blessing; hostility or opposition; culpability or moral condition; obligation, duty, liability, charge; addition or accompaniment; excess or comparison; pre-eminence or exaltation; [authority]; benefit; purpose; cause or ground; [specification]; [in accordance with/according to]; exchange; debt owed; temporal; instrumental; accompaniment; [concessive]; introducing object; *conjunction*: [causal]; [adversative]; [temporal]; [with various other words], pp. 6:385–98

Gesenius – locative; command; obligation; adversative, pp. 383–84 (§119aa–dd); causal clause with infinitive, pp. 348–49, 492 (§§114e, 158c)

Joüon & Muraoka – cause; excess; addition; proximity; pejorative; incumbency; *dativus incommodi*; emotive; simple dative, pp. 460–61 (§133f); causal and explicative clause, p. 600 (§170h); concessive clause, pp. 601–2 (§171a)

Van der Merwe – spatial; figurative extensions; direction to a goal; causal; norm; focus of attention; instrument, pp. 371–74 (§39.20)

Waltke & O'Connor – spatial; metaphorical; marks an object of excess; norm; oppositional; circumstance, pp. 216–18 (§11.2.13)

Williams – locative; terminative; disadvantage; concessive; specification; norm; causal; addition; accompaniment; obligated person; advantage; indirect object, pp. 112–15 (§§285–296)

עַל־כֵּן (156x)

HALOT, pp. 833–34; *Holladay*, p. 274

CONJUNCTIVE ADVERB
1. for that reason, therefore; so it happens that [logical consequence] [a]
2. כִּי־עַל־כֵּן seeing that (concessional) [b]
3. עַל אֲשֶׁר ... עַל־כֵּן because ... therefore [logical consequence] [c]

Arnold & Choi – statement of effect, p. 148 (§4.2.10b)
BDB – introducing statement of fact; origin of name, custom, or proverb, p. 487
DCH – [logical consequence], p. 4:433
Gesenius – causal clause, p. 492 (§158.b)
Joüon & Muraoka – causal and explicative clauses, p. 600 (§170h)
Van der Merwe – explanatory, pp. 450–52 (§40.38)
Waltke & O'Connor – statement of later effects, pp. 665–66 (§39.3.4e)

עַל(־)מֶה/עַל(־)מָה (18x)

see מָה in *HALOT*, p. 552; *Holladay*, p. 184

PREPOSITION
1. on what account?, on what basis?, why? [causal-interrogative] [D.5]

BDB – [causal-interrogative], p. 552
DCH – [causal-interrogative], p. 5:162
Gesenius – מָה with preposition, p. 443 (§137b)
Joüon & Muraoka – causal-interrogative, p. 600 (§170h)
Van der Merwe – inquires about the *reason* or *motivation* for a state of affairs or action, p. 480 (§42.3.7.4)

עַל־עֵקֶב (2x; Pss 40:16; 70:4)

see עֵקֶב in *HALOT*, p. 873; *Holladay*, p. 281

CONJUNCTION
1. on account of, really, as wages for [causal/exchange] [3]

BDB – consequence/causal, p. 784
DCH – [causal], p. 6:542

עַל־פְּנֵי (177x)

see פָּנֶה in *HALOT*, pp. 943–44; *Holladay*, p. 294

PREPOSITION
1. in the face of, in the sight of, before [spatial/positional/
   durational/relational] [D.8]
   a. on the surface [D.8.a]
   b. at the front of, before [D.8.b]
      • opposite, facing (in geographical descriptions)
   c. (with persons) [D.8.c]
      • before, in the sight of
      • before the eyes (meaning under the control of,
        during the lifetime of)
      • against, at the expensive of, to the disadvantage
        of (aggressively)
      • all over
   d. (in connection with God) [D.8.d]

BDB – [position]; [spatial], pp. 818–19
DCH – [spatial]; [position]; direction; of place; [disinterest/
   disadvantage: hostile action]; [correspondence], pp. 6:719–20

עִם (1,049x)

HALOT, pp. 839–40; *Holladay*, p. 275

PREPOSITION

1. in company with, together with [1]
   a. (in common) with [communal action] [1.a]
   b. (formula to express the divine presence) [1.b]
      - (as a promise and pledge) [1.b.i]
      - (in the mouth of people as a promise, pledge, wish, or question) [1.b.ii]
      - (. . . עִם (הָיָה) יהוה) (in retrospect) [1.b.iii]
      - (עִמָּנוּאֵל) [1.b.iv]
   c. (as statement of communality, even if it is one-sided, or antagonistic) [1.c]
   d. notwithstanding (adversative) [1.d]
2. [solidarity, comparative] [2]
   a. together with, as good as, as well as, just as much as [2.a]
   b. together with, even as [2.b]
   c. in comparison with [2.c]
3. simultaneously with, at the same time as [temporal] [3]
4. (with מִן) [4]
   a. from having a connection with (meaning forward from, from . . . to) [4.a]
   b. more than (comparative) [4.b]

Arnold & Choi – accompaniment; personal complement; locative; restrictive, pp. 136–37 (§4.1.17)

BDB – fellowship and companionship; aid; joint actions; contest or combat (hostile); dealing with or relation to a person; common lot; equality or resemblance (generally poetic); temporal; locative; of persons specifically: in the house, family, or service, possession, custody or care, exceptive, favor; idiomatically of thought or purpose; [concessive], pp. 767–69

DCH – *preposition*: accompaniment; possession; benefit; dealings with or action meted out to; dialogue or mutual agreement; conflict or dispute; thought, disposition or purpose; agreement; help; likeness; place; [exclusivity]; direction; time; instrumental; causal; [specification]; [adversative], introducing object; *conjunction*: [temporal]; with מִן, pp. 6:450–63

Gesenius – preposition of connection, p. 297 (§101a)

Van der Merwe – shared presence; possession; shared activity; recipient; support; devotion; addition, pp. 374–77 (§39.21)

Waltke & O'Connor – accompaniment; addition; end point; comparative, pp. 219–20 (§11.2.14)

Williams – accompaniment; locative; possessor; advantage; disadvantage; coordination; comparison; reciprocal; assistance; consciousness, pp. 125–27 (§§328–337)

עֵקֶב (15x)

HALOT, p. 873; *Holladay*, p. 281

CONJUNCTION
1. the very back, the end [substantive] [1]
2. result, wages, reward [substantive] [2]
3. עַל־עֵקֶב on account of, really, as wages for [causal/exchange] [3]
   • for the reason that (also עֵקֶב אֲשֶׁר and עֵקֶב כִּי)

Arnold & Choi – causal; reward; consequence, p. 192 (§5.2.5a)
BDB – [substantive]; consequence/causal; temporal, p. 784
DCH – [substantive]; [causal/exchange], p. 6:542
Hardy – substantive; causal, pp. 106–8 (§3.11.2.1–2)
Gesenius – causal; consequence, p. 492 (§158b)
Joüon & Muraoka – consequence; recompence; causal, p. 319 (§104b); causal and explicative clause, p. 600 (§170g)
Van der Merwe – causal, p. 434n66 (§40.29.1)

Waltke & O'Connor – causal; consequence, pp. 640–41 (§38.4a)
Williams – begins causal clause, p. 189 (§534)

וְעַתָּה/עַתָּה (433x)

HALOT, p. 902; *Holladay*, p. 287

ADVERB

1. now (at the present moment) [temporal] [1]
2. now [2]
   a. (in these circumstances/in the present situation) [2.a]
   b. (now it is apparent) [2.b]
3. (וְעַתָּה) [discourse marker] [3]
   a. and now (often introducing a new subject of section) [3.a]
   b. (under these conditions) [3.b]
   c. but now [3.c]
   d. from now on, henceforth [3.d]
   e. yet, nevertheless [3.e]
4. (עַד־עַתָּה) [temporal] [4]
   a. until now [4.a]
   b. until this time [4.b]
5. מֵעַתָּה from now on [temporal] [5]
6. (miscellaneous) [6]
   - לֹא עַתָּה no longer now
   - וְאַתָּה עַתָּה you now
   - עַתָּה זֶה so now, even now
   - מָה . . . עַתָּה so what . . . now?
   - הֲ . . . עַתָּה do you now have?
   - עַתָּה הַפַּעַם now at last
   - עַתָּה מְהֵרָה soon now
   - גַּם עַתָּה so now; וְגַם עַתָּה and now also
   - עַתָּה כְהַיּוֹם even today

135

- וְעַתָּה אֲשֶׁר and now it is that
- כִּי עַתָּה surely now, now then, but now

Arnold & Choi – temporal; logical, p. 151 (§4.2.14)
BDB – [temporal]; phrases, pp. 773–74
DCH – [temporal]; [discourse marker]; in rhetorical questions; idiomatic phrases, pp. 6:633–39
Joüon & Muraoka – determinate accusative of עֵת *time*, p. 258 (§93g)
Van der Merwe – discourse marker; simultaneous time; introducing main body of letter, pp. 452–54 (§40.39)
Waltke & O'Connor – stative temporal deictic, pp. 648, 663 (§39.3.1h, 4c); logical or emphatic, p. 667 (§39.3.4f)

פֹּה (57x)/פּוֹ (24x)/פֹּא (1x; Job 38:11)

HALOT, p. 916; *Holladay*, p. 289

ADVERB

1. (to) here, at this place [locative] [1]
2. to here [locative] [2]
3. מִפֹּו/פֹּה . . . מִפֹּו/פֹּה from here and there, meaning on both sides [3]
4. עַד־פֹּא as far as this [4]

BDB – locative, pp. 805–6
DCH – [locative], pp. 6:663–64
Joüon & Muraoka – demonstrative adverb, p. 306 (§102h)
Van der Merwe – adverb of place, p. 380 (§40.1.3.1a)
Waltke & O'Connor – adverb of location, p. 658 (§39.3.1g)

פֶּן (133x)

HALOT, pp. 936–37; *Holladay*, p. 293

CONJUNCTION

1. (with imperfect) [1]

    a. so that . . . not, lest (prevention of a theoretically possible event) [1.a]

    b. or else, in case, perhaps, otherwise (with imperfect) (rejection of a consequence which might be possible/ prevention of an otherwise predictable event) [1.b]

2. what else (מַה־פֶּן, without *maqqep* after פֶּן) [2]

3. otherwise (with perfect) [3]

4. (with יֵשׁ) [4]

Arnold & Choi – consequential, p. 166 (§4.3.5); negative final/result clauses, pp. 188–89 (§5.2.3c)

BDB – [negative result], pp. 814–15

DCH – [negative result], pp. 6:703–5

Gesenius – negative sentence, pp. 478–79, 482 (§152b, w)

Joüon & Muraoka – negative wish, pp. 596–97 (§168g)

Van der Merwe – negative purpose, pp. 467–69 (§41.11)

Waltke & O'Connor – negative final clauses, pp. 639–40, 660–61 (§§38.3c, 39.3.3a)

Williams – negative purpose, p. 163 (§461)

פְּנִימָה (13x)

HALOT, p. 945; *Holladay*, p. 294

ADVERB

1. into, (to the) inside [spatial] [1]

2. within, inside [spatial] [2]

3. לִפְנִימָה into, inside, (to the) inside, inwards [spatial] [3]

    • מִפְּנִימָה on the inside

BDB – [spatial], p. 819

DCH – [spatial], p. 6:721

Waltke & O'Connor – adverb of location, p. 658 (§39.3.1g)

פִּתְאֹם (24x)/פִּתְאוֹם (1x; Ps 64:8)

HALOT, pp. 983–84; *Holladay*, p. 300

ADVERB

    1. suddenly, surprisingly [manner]

        a. (element of surprise) [a]

        b. פֶּתַע פִּתְאֹם quite suddenly, all of a sudden [b]

            • פִּתְאֹם לְפֶתַע in no time at all, in a flash, really as quick as the blink of an eye, in an instant

            • פַּחַד פִּתְאֹם sudden panic, sudden terror

BDB – *substantive*; *adverbial accusative* [of manner], p. 837

DCH – [*substantive*]; *adverb* [of manner], p. 6:797

Gesenius – [manner], p. 295 (§100g)

Joüon & Muraoka – [manner], p. 303 (§102b)

Van der Merwe – manner, p. 380 (§40.1.3.1b)

Waltke & O'Connor – manner adverb, p. 659 (§39.3.1j)

Williams – [manner], p. 137 (§377)

פֶּתַע (7x)

HALOT, pp. 990–91; *Holladay*, p. 301

ADVERB

    1. a moment, an instant [substantive] [a]

    2. instantly, immediately (time/manner) [b]

BDB – *substantive*; *adverbial accusative* [of manner], p. 837

DCH – [*substantive*]; *adverb* [of manner], p. 812

Gesenius – [manner], p. 295 (§100g)

Joüon & Muraoka – [manner], p. 305 (§102d)

Waltke & O'Connor – manner adverb, p. 659 (§39.3.1j)

קְדֹרַנִּית (1x; Mal 3:14)

HALOT, p. 1072; *Holladay*, p. 313

ADVERB

> 1. with a long face, unkempt, dressed in mourning attire [manner]

BDB – adverb [of manner], p. 871
DCH – adverb [of manner], p. 7:190
Gesenius – [manner], p. 295 (§100g)
Joüon & Muraoka – manner, p. 304 (§102b)

קוֹמְמִיּוּת (1x; Lev 26:13)

HALOT, p. 1089; *Holladay*, p. 316

ADVERB

> 1. in an upright position, (walk) erect, with head high [metaphorical]

BDB – adverb, p. 879
DCH – adverb, p. 7:236

רֹאשׁ(וֹ)ן (180x)/רִישׁוֹן (1x; Job 8:8)/ רִאישׁוֹן (1x; Job 15:7)

HALOT, pp. 1168–69; *Holladay*, pp. 329–30

ADVERB

> 1. first [1]
>> a. the first in rank, in a series [1.a]
>> b. the first in contrast to the second [1.b]
>> c. the first month, the first days [1.c]
>> d. (adverbial) [1.d]

- (temporal) בָּרִאשֹׁ(וֹ)נָה for the first time, the first time before, רִאשֹׁ(וֹ)נָה first, בָּרִאשֹׁ(וֹ)נָה first, כְּבָרִאשֹׁנָה = כְּרִאשֹׁנָה like the first time [1.d.i]

- (place) first and foremost, יָשַׁב רִאשֹׁנָה to occupy the first position, בָּרִאשֹׁנָה in first position [1.d.ii]

e. כָּעֵת הָרִאשׁוֹן like the previous time [1.e]

  - הָרִאשׁוֹן ... וְהָאַחֲרוֹן meaning everyone, from first to last

f. הָרִאשׁוֹן the first to state his case [1.f]

2. earlier, former [2]

3. (miscellaneous) [3]

BDB – adjective; adverb, pp. 911–12

DCH – adjective; adverb, pp. 7:377–81

Gesenius – ordinal, p. 292 (§98.a)

Joüon & Muraoka – adjective used in the adverbial sense, p. 304 (§102c)

Waltke & O'Connor – common primary ordinal, p. 284 (§15.3.1a)

רַבָּה/(3x; Pss 62:3; 78:15; 89:8) רַבַּת (5x)

see רַב in *HALOT*, p. 1172; *Holladay*, p. 330

ADVERB

1. (adverbial רַבַּת) [8]

  a. in rich measure, abundantly [degree], too long (a time) [temporal] [8.a]

  b. רַבָּה much, very [degree] [8.b]

BDB – [degree]; [temporal], p. 913

DCH – [degree]; [temporal], p. 7:385

Gesenius – [degree], p. 295 (§100d)
Waltke & O'Connor – temporal adverb; adverb of degree,
  pp. 658–59 (§39.3.1h, i)

רֶ֫גַע (22x)

HALOT, p. 1189; *Holladay*, p. 333

ADVERB
1. quiet, calm period of time [substantive] [1]
2. duration, period [substantive] [2]
   • רֶגַע . . . רֶגַע one moment . . . the next
3. a short while, a trice, moment, instant, suddenly [3]
4. in a trice, abruptly, every moment (temporal accusative) [4]
5. לִרְגָעִים again and again [5]

BDB – [*substantive*]; *adverbial accusative*, p. 921
DCH – [*substantive*]; [*adverb*], p. 7:417
Waltke & O'Connor – manner adverb, p. 659 (§39.3.1j)

רֵיקָם (16x)

HALOT, p. 1229; *Holladay*, p. 339

ADVERB
1. with empty hands, i.e., without a gift [manner] [1]
2. without success, plunder [manner] [2]
3. without possessions, property, family [manner] [3]
4. without cause [manner] [4]
5. (various expressions) [5]

BDB – *adverb* [of manner], p. 938
DCH – *adverb* [of manner], p. 7:485

Gesenius – [manner], p. 295 (§100g)
Joüon & Muraoka – [manner], p. 303 (§102b)
Van der Merwe – manner adverb, p. 381 (§40.1.3.1.2a)
Waltke & O'Connor – manner adverb, p. 659 (§39.3.1j)

רְמִיָּה (1x; Jer 48:10)

HALOT, pp. 1243–44; *Holladay*, p. 340

ADVERB

  1. to do something slackly, negligently [manner] [A.2]

BDB – [*substantive*], p. 941
DCH – [*substantive*]; *adverb*, p. 7:498

רַק (109x)

see II רַק in *HALOT*, pp. 1286–88; *Holladay*, p. 346

ADVERB

  1. (within a clause) [1]
    a. only (without any negating preposition) (exclusive) [1.a]
    b. apart from (following the negating particle אַיִן or אֵין) (emphatic) [1.b]
  2. (at the beginning of a sentence) [2]
    a. only (refers to the following word) [2.a]
    b. only, just (refers to a following verbal clause) [2.b]
      • (before an imperative) [2.b.i]
      • only, however (before אַל with jussive) (adversative) [2.b.ii]
      • only, still, but, however, nevertheless (before the imperfect or jussive as a statement, command, or prohibition, expresses something

which either contradicts or varies from that which precedes it) [2.b.iii]
- only, but (before the perfect) [2.b.iv]
- (after perfect consecutive) [2.b.v]
- only (with participle) [2.b.vi]

c. only (in clauses in which the verb is implicitly presupposed) [2.c]

d. surely, only, however, even so (in a nominal clause) [2.d]

3. (misc. and particular instances) [3]
- רַק־הַפַּעַם only this once
- רַק לְמַעַן only so that
- רַק בְּעֵינֶיךָ תַבִּיט yes, you may see it with your own eyes
- לְעֵת מְצֹא רַק literally in the moment of finding

Arnold & Choi – restrictive, asseverative, pp. 151–52 (§4.2.15); exceptive clause, p. 193 (§5.2.7); restrictive clause, p. 194 (§5.2.8); asseverative clauses, p. 203 (§5.3.3d)

BDB – restrictive; limitative; emphasizing; after a negative; with affirmative, asseverative force; רַק אִם (רַק prefixed for emphasis), p. 956

DCH – [restrictive]; [exceptive]; [limitative]; [adversative]; affirmative; in particular combinations, pp. 7:549–50

Gesenius – restrictive and intensive clauses, p. 483 (§153)

Joüon & Muraoka – asseverative clause, pp. 580–81 (§164a)

Van der Merwe – limitation with a countering effect; conviction as to the correctness of an observation or evaluation, pp. 455–56 (§40.41)

Waltke & O'Connor – restrictive adverb, pp. 669–70 (§39.3.5c)

Williams – restrictive; asseverative; exception to a negative; emphatic, pp. 141–42 (§§390–393)

שַׁ/שֶׁ (שַׁ/שֶׁ if doubling is impossible, or if it would result in e-a, e-ō) (138x)

see שַׁ in *HALOT*, pp. 1365–66 (for uses see אֲשֶׁר, pp. 50–51); *Holladay*, p. 356

RELATIVE PARTICLE
1. (for the usage see אֲשֶׁר in the relative) [1]
   a. (a linking particle following the substantive/ introducing a nominal clause after noun) [1.a]
      - שֶׁלִּי which is mine (i.e., my)
      - בְּשֶׁלִּי (equivalent to בִּי) it is on my account
      - בְּשֶׁלְּמִי on whose account
   b. (precedes a relative clause, like אֲשֶׁר) [1.b]
      - (introducing a verbal clause) [1.b.α]
      - (in a generalizing sense, with prefixed מַה־) [1.b.β]
   c. which (in a complex relative clause) [1.c]
      - (on the day) when [temporal]
      - wherein (שָׁם ... שֶׁ or שֶׁשָּׁם)
      - (with prefixed כְּ)
   d. that (after verb of saying, knowing, etc.) [nominalizing] [1.d]
      - עַד שֶׁ until that [temporal]
      - שֶׁגַּם even that, that also [asseverative/additive]
   e. since, because [causal] [1.e]

Arnold & Choi – relative particle, p. 172 (§4.6.2); relative clause, pp. 197–99 (§5.2.13).

BDB – relative pronoun; connecting link; *conjunction*: [nominalizing]; reason; compounds, pp. 979–80

DCH – relative pronoun; [independent relative]; *conjunction*: [nominalizing]; [epexegetical]; result; comparative; [reason]; [temporal]; [introduces an apodosis preceding a conditional clause]; compounds, pp. 8:201–4

Gesenius – shares the same syntactic and semantic features of אֲשֶׁר; the relative pronoun, pp. 112, 444–47 (§§36, 138); *conjunction*, p. 306 (§104b); interrogative pronoun, p. 445 (§137c); the noun–clause, pp. 454–55 (§141n); relative clause, pp. 485–89 (§155); circumstantial clause, p. 489 (§156b); object clause, pp. 491–92 (§157); causal clause, p. 492 (§158b); comparative clause, p. 499 (§161b); temporal clause, pp. 502–5 (§164d, f); final clause, p. 504 (§165b); consecutive clause, p. 505 (§166b).

Joüon & Muraoka – relative pronoun, p. 108 (§38); subordinating conjunction, p. 319 (§104a); relative clause, pp. 443, 557–64 (§§129q; 158); abbreviation of אֲשֶׁר, pp. 503–4 (§145b)

Van der Merwe – relative complementizer; independent relative; zero relative; resumptive; complement after verbs of observation; mental processes or speech; result; purpose; cause; motivation; real condition, p. 307 (§36.3.2)

Waltke & O'Connor – introduces dependent or attributive relative clauses; temporal; locative; independent relative; vocative, pp. 335–36 (§19.4)

Williams – relative; nominalizing; result; causal, pp. 167–68 (§§470–474)

שָׁוְא (52x)/שׁוּ (1x; Job 15:31)

HALOT, pp. 1425–26; *Holladay*, pp. 361–62

ADVERB

1. (in certain contexts) [4]
   a. worthless, meaning futile, in vain [4.a]
   b. הָיָה שָׁוְא to come to nothing [4.b]
   c. אַךְ־שָׁוְא it is all to no purpose [4.c]
   • שָׁוְא with infinitive, it is purposeless to

BDB – [*substantive*]; *adverb*, p. 996

DCH – [*substantive*]; [*adverb*], pp. 8:271–72
Waltke & O'Connor – manner adverb, p. 659 (§39.3.1j)

שִׁלְשׁוֹם (24x)

HALOT, pp. 1545–46; *Holladay*, p. 374

ADVERB

   1. three days ago, the day before yesterday (always in combination as idiom, meaning up to now) [1]

     a. תְּמוֹל שִׁלְשֹׁ(וֹ)ם yesterday and the day before that, meaning previously [1.a]

     b. כִּתְמֹ(וֹ)ל שִׁלְשֹׁ(וֹ)ם as yesterday and as the day before that, meaning as previously [1.b]

     c. מִתְמֹ(וֹ)ל שִׁלְשֹׁ(וֹ)ם since yesterday and since the day before that, meaning for some time [1.c]

     d. גַּם־אֶתְמוֹל גַּם־שִׁלְשׁוֹם, גַּם־תְּמוֹל גַּם־שִׁלְשֹׁ(וֹ)ם as well as yesterday also the day before that, meaning: for some considerable time [1.d]

     e. גַּם מִתְּמוֹל גַּם מִשִּׁלְשֹׁם at any time at all (in a negative clause) [1.e]

BDB – *adverb*: [temporal], p. 1026
DCH – *adverb*: [temporal], pp. 8:415–16
Joüon & Muraoka – [temporal], p. 304 (§102b)
Waltke & O'Connor – temporal adverb, p. 658 (§39.3.1h)
Williams – [temporal], p. 137 (§377)

שָׁם (locative שָׁמָּה) (834x)

HALOT, pp. 1546–48; *Holladay*, p. 374

ADVERB

   1. [locative] [1]

a. there, over there, (to) there [1.a]

- אֲשֶׁר שָׁם where, (to) where
- שָׁם ... שָׁם here ... there

2. (temporal) [2]

a. then, at that time, just then [2.a]

3. (with either local or temporal significance) [3]

4. (with preposition: מִשָּׁם) [4]

a. from there, from these [4.a]

- אֲשֶׁר מִשָּׁם from where

b. (locative or temporal) [4.b]

- from over there [4.b.α]
- from thence [4.b.β]

c. (used with a preposition in a subordinate clause) [4.c]

- from which (place) [4.c.α]
- from which (referring to הָאֲדָמָה) [4.c.β]
- out of it, from it (referring to flour and oil) [4.c.γ]

5. שָׁמָּה [5]

a. (to) there [terminative] [5.a]

b. there [5.b]

c. אֲשֶׁר שָׁמָּה (to) where, whither, where [5.c]

6. (various other instances) [6]

a. שָׁם meaning look! [6.a]

Arnold & Choi – locative; terminative, pp. 152–53 (§4.2.16)

BDB – [locative]; [terminative]; with locative ה, p. 1027

DCH – [locative]; [terminative]; time, pp. 8:417–22

Gesenius – place; time, p. 294 (§100a)

Joüon & Muraoka – demonstrative adverb, pp. 305–6 (§102h)

Van der Merwe – place, p. 380 (§40.1.3.1a)

Waltke & O'Connor – adverb of location; temporal adverb, p. 658 (§39.3.1g, h)

תַּחַת — שְׁנִים/שֵׁנִית

שֵׁנִית (20x)/שְׁנִים (1x; Num 2:16)

see שֵׁנִי in *HALOT*, pp. 1604–5; *Holladay*, p. 379

ADVERB

    1. for the second time [temporal/order] [1.a]

BDB – [adverb], p. 1041
DCH – adverb, pp. 8:506–7
Gesenius – adverb, p. 295 (§100f)
Joüon & Muraoka – ordinal number used adverbially,
    p. 305 (§102f)

תַּחַת (505x)

HALOT, pp. 1721–23; *Holladay*, p. 389

PREPOSITION

    1. what is located underneath, below (substantive) [1]
        a. תַּחַת הָהָר at the foot of the mountain [1.a]
        b. תַּחְתָּיו, תַּחְתָּו in his place (meaning, where he
        stood) [1.b]
    2. preposition [2]
        a. below, underneath, under [locative/metaphorical]
        [2.a]
        • subdued under
        • under (the authority of)
        b. (seek protection) under (2.b)
        • under (the tongue); under (the lips)
        c. (of animals) [2.c]
    3. in place of, instead of [exchange] [3]
        a. in place of [3.a]
        b. as recompense for [3.b]
        • instead of (with infinitive)
    4. (with particles) [4]

148

a. אֶל־תַּחַת going underneath (with verbs of motion) [4.a]

b. תַּחַת אֲשֶׁר instead of [4.b]

c. תַּחַת כִּי for the reason that [4.c]

d. תַּחַת לְ on the lower side of [4.d]

e. מִתַּחַת [4.e]

- from underneath [4.e.α]
- from out of its place [4.e.β]
- away from its place [4.e.γ]
- מִתַּחַת לְ on the lower side of, below [4.e.δ]

ADVERB

1. מִתַּחַת [4.f]

a. lying underneath, below [locative] [4.f.α]

b. מִתַּחַת לְ below [4.f.β]

c. לְמִתַּחַת לְ below [4.f.γ]

d. עַד־מִתַּחַת לְ as far as below [4.f.δ]

Arnold & Choi – vertical relationship; static position; metaphorical; substitution, pp. 137–38 (§4.1.18)

BDB – *adverbial accusative*: [locative]; *preposition*: [locative]; in transferred sense; *conjunction*: [exchange]; [causal]; compounds, pp. 1065–66

DCH – *preposition*: [locative]; authority; [metaphorical]; [exchange]; [representative]; [manner]; compounds; *adverb*: [locative]; *conjunction*: [causal]; [concessive]; [combined with interrogative], pp. 8:621–27

Gesenius – spatial preposition, p. 297 (§101a); causal clause, p. 492 (§158b)

Hardy – spatial; substitutive; causal; subjugative, pp. 110–13 (§3.12.2–7)

Van der Merwe – vertical space below; control; substitution; exchange; causation, pp. 377–78 (§39.22)

Waltke & O'Connor – locational; authority or control, p. 220
   (§11.2.15); causal clause, pp. 640–41 (§38.4)
Williams – locative; authority; identity of situation; exchange;
   introduce a causal clause, pp. 129–31 (§§348–353)

תָּמִיד (104x)

HALOT, pp. 1747–48; *Holladay*, p. 391

ADVERB
   1. lasting, continually [1]
   2. (substantivized adjective in construct expressions as
   nomen rectum) [2]

Arnold & Choi – manner, p. 153
BDB – *adverb*; *substantive*, p. 556
DCH – [*substantive*]; *adverb*, pp. 8:641–43
Waltke & O'Connor – *adverb of identity of action*, p. 659
   (§39.3.1i)

INTERPRETIVE
ARAMAIC LEXICON

Analysis of Adverbs, Conjunctions,
Interjections, Particles,
Prepositions, and Pronouns

אֱדַיִן (57x) (Heb. אָז/אֲזַי)

HALOT, p. 1807; Holladay, p. 396

ADVERB
1. then [temporal]

BDB – at beginning of sentence, introducing new stage of narrative with some emphasis [discourse marker], p. 1078

Cook – temporal deictic adverb, p. 216 (§350a); discourse marker (introduces new events into a narrative), p. 262 (§431a)

Rosenthal – coordinating conjunction, p. 42 (§85); temporal demonstrative adverb, p. 44 (§89)

Vogt – temporal; [discourse marker]; inferential, pp. 25–26

אַדְרַזְדָּא (1x; Ezra 7:23)

HALOT, p. 1807; Holladay, p. 396

ADVERB
1. careful devotion, diligently, zealously [manner]

BDB – [manner], p. 1079
Cook – manner adverb, p. 218 (§351d)
Rosenthal – modal assertive adverb, p. 44 (§93)
Vogt – [manner], p. 26

אֲחֲרֵי/אַחֹר (3x; Dan 2:29, 45; 7:24) (Heb. אַחֹר/אַחֲרֵי)

HALOT, p. 1810; Holladay, pp. 396–97

PREPOSITION
1. after [temporal]

BDB – [temporal], p. 1079
Cook – temporal, p. 132 (§190)
Rosenthal – temporal, p. 40 (§84)
Vogt – substantive; *adverb*: [temporal]; [logical]; inferential,
at the beginning of an apodosis; *preposition*: [temporal];
spatial, pp. 29–30

אַחֲרֵי דְנָה (2x; Dan 2:29, 45)

HALOT, pp. 1810, 1854; *Holladay*, pp. 396–97, 402

PREPOSITION
1. after this [temporal]

BDB – [temporal], pp. 1079, 1089
Cook – temporal, p. 132 (§190)
Vogt – [temporal], pp. 30, 101

אָחֲרֵין (1x; Dan 4:5)

HALOT, p. 1810; *Holladay*, p. 397

ADVERB
1. at last, finally [temporal]

BDB – [temporal], p. 1079
Cook – temporal adverb, p. 70 (§116)
Rosenthal – temporal demonstrative adverb, p. 44 (§89)
Vogt – [temporal], p. 29

אֲתִי/אִיתַי (17x) (Heb. יֵשׁ, also אִשׁ)

HALOT, pp. 1811–12; *Holladay*, p. 397

PARTICLE

1. he is nothing, he possesses nothing, he has nothing, there is, are [existence] [1]
2. with לֹא: there is not [negative existence] [2]
3. (with a suffix) [existence] [3]
   a. there is [3.a]
      - with לָא there is not
   b. to be found [3.b]
   c. (with הֵן): [3.c]
      - הֵן אִיתַי דִי whether it be so that
      - as a stressed copula before a participle or adjective
   d. (elsewhere with suffix) [3.d]
      - (with pleonastic suffix)

BDB – [particle of existence], p. 1080

Cook – emphasis, p. 193 (§315); existential predicator of existence; existence *simpliciter*, pp. 233–35 (§380)

Rosenthal – particle of existence; with negation; may take the place of the copula for emphasis, p. 45 (§95)

Vogt – denoting presence in a place; equals a more or less emphatic *copula*, pp. 32–34

אַל (3x; Dan 2:24; 4:16; 5:10) (same in Heb.)

HALOT, pp. 1812–13; *Holladay*, p. 397

ADVERB

1. not (prohibitive)

BDB – prohibitive, p. 1080

Cook – used only to negate jussives, p. 239 (§388)

Rosenthal – used with the jussive to express a negative wish or command, p. 43 (§87)

Vogt – prohibition or negative wish, pp. 34–35

אֱלוּ (5x)

HALOT, p. 1814; *Holladay*, p. 397

INTERJECTION
> **1.** (mostly considered as a by-form of אֲרוּ) [a]
> **2.** look! behold! [b]

BDB – interjection (usually regarded as a by-form of אֲרוּ)
(always in a description of a vision), p. 1080
Cook – presentative construction, p. 237 (§384)
Rosenthal – local demonstrative adverb, p. 44 (§91)
Vogt – interjection that introduces a clause about a new
topic, pp. 36–37

אָסְפַּרְנָא (7x)

HALOT, pp. 1820–21; *Holladay*, p. 398

ADVERB
> **1.** completely, exactly [manner]

BDB – [manner], p. 1082
Cook – manner, p. 218 (§351d)
Rosenthal – modal assertive adverb, p. 44 (§93)
Vogt – [manner], pp. 46–47

אַף (4x) (Heb. I אַף)

HALOT, pp. 1821–22; *Holladay*, p. 398

CONJUNCTION
> **1.** also, always linked with וְ (וְאַף) and also [additive]

BDB – [additive], p. 1082

Cook – discourse marker: gives additional or summary material relevant to a preceding topic; less frequently, it modifies particular words in a sentence, p. 262 (§432)

Rosenthal – modal assertive adverb, p. 44 (§93)

Vogt – adding simply something new; in narrative and counting; emphasizing, pp. 47–48

אַפְּתֹם (1x; Ezra 4:13)

HALOT, p. 1823; *Holladay*, p. 398

ADVERB
1. surely, certainly, eventually, positively (meaning of the word is uncertain) [asseverative]

BDB – of uncertain meaning, p. 1082

Rosenthal – modal assertive adverb, p. 44 (§93)

Vogt – [manner], pp. 48–49

אֲרוּ (5x)

HALOT, pp. 1823–24; *Holladay*, p. 398

INTERJECTION
1. look! behold!

BDB – interjection, p. 1082

Cook – presentative construction, p. 237 (§384)

Rosenthal – local demonstrative adverb, p. 44 (§91)

Vogt – interjection that introduces a clause about a new topic, pp. 36–37

בְּ

בְּ (226x) (the same as in Heb.)

HALOT, p. 1830; *Holladay*, p. 399

PREPOSITION
1. in [1]
   a. in (spatial, place where) [locative] [1.a]
   b. in (meaning according to, corresponding to)
      [in accordance with/according to] [1.b]
2. into, in, on to, from, about (spatial, place to which)
   [directional] [2]
3. בְּעִדָּנָא דִי when, as soon as (temporal) [3]
4. through, by means of (instrumental) [4]
   • for (the price of) [exchange]
5. with (concomitant circumstances) [5]
6. (other expressions) [6]
   a. with other verbs [6.a]
      • שְׁתָה בְּ to drink from
      • הֵימִין בְּ to trust in
      • שְׁלֵט בְּ to rule over
      • עֲבַד בְּ to treat, deal with
   b. יוֹם בְּיוֹם day by day [6.b]
7. (composite expressions) [7]

BDB – place; time; [spatial]; instrumental; price [exchange];
   [causal]; [specification]; after verbs of ruling, trusting,
   looking at, p. 1083

Cook – location in or near a physical space; accompaniment;
   position in time; figurative location with nouns of subjective
   experience; instrument or the means of carrying out an
   action; role or position that something has; marking reciprocal participants; temporal distribution; general association;
   marking verbal complements, pp. 121–23 (§§179–180)

Rosenthal – local; temporal; instrumental; with suffixes,
   p. 38 (§77)

Vogt – [locative]; [directional]; [temporal]; expressing instrument, cause, etc.; modal; [specification]; price [exchange]; [in accordance with/according to]; variations, pp. 59–65

בֵּאדַיִן (29x)

see אֱדַיִן in *HALOT*, p. 1807; *Holladay*, p. 396

ADVERB
1. then [temporal]

BDB – [temporal], p. 1078
Cook – temporal deictic adverb, p. 216 (§350.a); discourse marker (introduces new events into a narrative), p. 262 (§431.a)
Rosenthal – coordinating conjunction, p. 42 (§85); temporal demonstrative adverb, p. 44 (§89)
Vogt – temporal; [discourse marker], pp. 25–26

בְּתַר/בָּאתַר (3x; Dan 2:39; 7:6, 7)

HALOT, p. 1831; *Holladay*, p. 399

PREPOSITION
1. after [temporal]

BDB – [temporal], p. 1083
Cook – temporal; locative, p. 132 (§191)
Rosenthal – temporal, p. 40 (§84)
Vogt – [temporal]; locative, p. 59

בָּאתַר דְּנָה (2x; Dan 7:6, 7)

HALOT, pp. 1831, 1854; *Holladay*, p. 402

PREPOSITION
1. after this [temporal]

BDB – [temporal], pp. 1083, 1089
Cook – temporal, p. 132 (§191)
Rosenthal – temporal, p. 40 (§84)
Vogt – [temporal], pp. 59, 101

בְּגוֹא (6x) (Heb. II גַּו)

see גַּו in *HALOT*, p. 1843; *Holladay*, p. 401

PREPOSITION
1. in, in the middle of [spatial] [a]

BDB – [spatial], p. 1086
Cook – [spatial], p. 121 (§179b)
Vogt – [spatial], p. 81

בֵּין (2x; Dan 7:5, 8) (same in Heb.)

HALOT, pp. 1832–33; *Holladay*, p. 399

PREPOSITION
1. between [spatial]

BDB – [spatial], p. 1084
Cook – [spatial], p. 133 (§194)
Rosenthal – [spatial], p. 40 (§84)
Vogt – [spatial]; [temporal], pp. 67–68

בְּרַם (5x)

HALOT, p. 1840; *Holladay*, p. 400

CONJUNCTION
1. except what, yet, but, however [adversative]

BDB – adversative, p. 1085
Cook – marks the B-clause as adversative, limiting the
   application of the A-clause, p. 245 (§396)
Rosenthal – [adversative], p. 42 (§85)
Vogt – [adversative], p. 78

דהוא (*ketiv* דְּהוּא and *qere* דְּהָיֵא)
(1x; Ezra 4:9) (but read דִּי־הוּא)

HALOT, p. 1849; *Holladay*, p. 401

COMPOUND PRONOUN
1. דִּי־הוּא that is [epexegetical]

BDB – [epexegetical], p. 1087

דִּי (344x)/דִּי (1x; Dan 3:15)

HALOT, pp. 1850–51; *Holladay*, p. 402

DEMONSTRATIVE PARTICLE (Heb. זוּ, זֶה)
1. (expresses a genitive relationship) [1]
   • (after a determinate noun)
   • (after an indeterminate noun)
   • (if both nouns are determinate, often with a
     proleptic suffix; e.g., דִּי־אֱלָהָא שְׁמֵהּ his name,
     i.e., God's)
   • of (to identify the material with which something
     is made)

RELATIVE PARTICLE (Heb. שֶׁ, אֲשֶׁר)

1. (introducing a relative clause) [2]
   a. which, who (following a noun) [2.a]
   b. (as an explicitly expressed subject) [2.b]
   c. that which, what (as an object) [2.c]
      - כָּל־דִּי everything that
      - דִּי־שְׁמֵהּ whose name (followed by noun with suffix)
      - בְּעִדָּנָא דִּי as soon as [temporal]
      - דִּי־הִיא that is (followed by personal pronoun)
      - דִּי אִנִּין which are
   d. (after an interrogative pronoun) [2.d]
      - מַן־דִּי who
      - מָה/א דִּי that which (Heb. מִי אֲשֶׁר, מַה־שֶּׁ)
   e. דִּי . . . תַּמָּה where [2.e.α]
      - דִּי לֵהּ־הִיא which are his
      - דִּי־לָא תִתְחַבַּל indestructible (with infinitive) [2.e.β]
      - לְהַשְׁנָיָה דִּי־לָא irrevocable
      - דִּי־לָא without
      - דִּי־לָא בִידַיִן without human assistance

CONJUNCTION (Heb. אֲשֶׁר, כִּי)

1. that (after a verb of knowing, announcing, seeing, hearing, recognizing, requesting, ordering, introducing permission, following עֲתִיד) [nominalizing] [3.a]
   - עֲתִיד דִּי ready to
   - מִן־קְשֹׁט דִּי it belongs to the truth that, i.e., truly
   - דִּי(וְ) whereas
   - כָּל־קֳבֵל דִּי just as
2. (introducing direct speech) (like ὅτι) [3.b]
3. so that, in order that (with final clause) [3.c]
   - דִּי־לְמָה and דִּי לָא so that . . . not, lest
4. so that (in consecutive clauses) [3.d]

5. for, because (causal) [3.e]
6. (with prepositions) [3.f]
   a. כְּדִי as, when (Heb. כַּאֲשֶׁר) [3.f.α]
   b. מִן־דִּי after; as soon as, to the extent that; because [3.f.β]
   c. for עַל/־ד דְּבָרַת דִּי, see further דִּבְרָה [3.f.γ]
   - for עַד־דִּי, see further עַד
   - for כָּל־קֳבֵל דִּי and לָקֳבֵל דִּי, see further קֳבֵל

BDB – relative pronoun; as mark of the genitive; *conjunction*: [nominalizing]; [causal], purpose; prefixed to direct narration; with other prepositions and prefixes, pp. 1087–88

Cook – *relative pronoun*: pronominal substitute; resumptive; restrictive and non-restrictive; independent relative; topical elements, pp. 84, 92–95, 277 (§§135, 148.a, b, c, 149, 150, 370); *genitive exponent*: pronominal possessive; periphrastic; genitive of material (also used in a quasi-adjectival manner); anticipates a dependent nominal, pp. 100–104 (§§159, 160–62); *conjunction*: purpose; causal, pp. 247–49, 251 (§§400–404, 409); *complementizer*: direct object of verbs of perceiving, knowing, or saying; introducing direct discourse; [nominalizing], pp. 258–59 (§§426b, 427)

Rosenthal – [nominalizing]; final clauses; causal; direct speech; temporal, p. 42 (§86)

Vogt – *demonstrative particle; substitute for the genitive*: after determined noun; before a genitive of quality or material; *relative particle*: a complete clause follows; as object of a clause; as subject of a clause; substantivized relative pronoun; in an indefinite relative clause; in an adverbial relative clause denoting time or place; *conjunction*: [nominalizing]; introducing direct discourse; introducing a clause that takes up a topic already mentioned and completes the sense of the main clause; causal; with imperfect after verbs of asking, commanding, etc.; with the imperfect expressing purpose; in composite conjunctions, pp. 88–97

דִּי־לָא (8x when used as a compound)

see דִּי in *HALOT*, p. 1851; *Holladay* p. 402

PARTICLE

1. without [privative] [2.e.β]
   - דִּי־לָא תִתְהֲבַל indestructible (with infinitive)
   - דִּי־לָא לְהַשְׁנָיָה irrevocable
   - דִּי־לָא בִידַיִן without human assistance

CONJUNCTION

1. so that . . . not, lest [negative purpose] [3.c]

BDB – [privative]; [negative purpose], pp. 1087–88
Cook – quasi-prepositional negation, p. 238 (§386f); modal, negative purpose, pp. 198, 247–48 (§§322, 401b, 402c)
Rosenthal – negations, p. 43 (§87)
Vogt – [privative], p. 189

הָ/הֲ (6x) (same in Heb.)

HALOT, p. 1856; *Holladay*, p. 403

INTERROGATIVE

1. (always proclitic, before first word of questions) (interrogative particle)
   - הַצְדָּא is it true?

BDB – interrogative particle, p. 1089
Cook – polar questions, expected positive answer, pp. 239–40 (§390)

Rosenthal – interrogative particle, p. 45 (§94)
Vogt – prefixed interrogative particle, p. 103

הָא (1x; Dan 3:25) (Heb. הֵא)

HALOT, p. 1856; *Holladay*, p. 403

INTERJECTION
   1. look!, see!, behold! [emphasizing]

BDB – interjection, p. 1089
Cook – presentative; emphasis, pp. 236–37 (§383)
Rosenthal – local demonstrative adverb, p. 44 (§91)
Vogt – interjection, p. 103

הָא (1x; Dan 2:43) (Heb. אֵיךְ, הֵיךְ)

HALOT, p. 1856; *Holladay*, p. 403

INTERJECTION
   1. הָא־כְדִי just as [manner]

BDB – prefixed idiom to כְ for greater definiteness, p. 1089
Cook – introduces a manner clause, p. 253 (§416)
Rosenthal – [manner], p. 42 (§86)
Vogt – [manner], p. 103

הֵן (16x) (Heb. אִם)

HALOT, p. 1861; *Holladay*, p. 404

PREPOSITION
   1. if [conditional protasis] [1]
     • הֵן לָא if not, הֵן . . . לָא if not

- הֲ ... הֲ ... הֲ whether ... or ... or
2. whether (in a dependent question) [alternative] [2]

BDB – [conditional]; הֲ repeated [alternative]; in indirect
question, p. 1090
Cook – conditional protasis; concessive; possible result;
alternative, pp. 256–57 (§422a–d)
Rosenthal – [conditional protasis], [alternative], p. 42 (§86)
Vogt – introducing a conditional clause; introducing an
indirect question with the idea of expectation or attempt;
in a disjunction; as enclitic, pp. 113–14

הֵן אִיתַי דִּי (1x; Ezra 5:17)

see אִיתַי in *HALOT*, p. 1812; *Holladay*, p. 397

PARTICLE
1. whether it be so that [existential] [3.c]

BDB – [existential], p. 1080
Cook – introduces an existential clause, p. 235 (§380g)
Vogt – הֵן introduces an indirect question with the idea of
expectation or attempt; subject is a clause introduced by
דִּי, to which אִיתַי gives emphasis, pp. 33, 113–14

וְ (729x) (Heb. וְ)

HALOT, pp. 1862–63; *Holladay*, p. 404

CONJUNCTION
1. and that, and specifically [specifying addition] [a]
2. and also (intensifying) [b]
3. but (adversative) [c]
4. or [alternative] [d]

5. for (explanatory) [e]
6. then, so (continuous) [f]
   • (often to be omitted in translation after imperative)
7. in order that (purpose) [g]

BDB – connecting words and sentences; [specifying addition]; contrastive; [continuous]; intention [purpose]; introducing the predicate, pp. 1090–91

Cook – simple coordination; consequence; purpose; parallel; desire and fulfillment; adversative; circumstantial; action-result, pp. 243–44, 249–50 (§§393, 405); conditional, p. 256 (§422a)

Rosenthal – coordinating conjunction connecting words and sentences, p. 41 (§85)

Vogt – polysyndetic joins; completing an enumeration; [specifying addition]; [continuous]; [asseverative/epexegetical]; [adversative]; [alternative]; consequence or conclusion; purpose clause; object or subject clause [nominalizing]; modal; circumstantial; introducing apodosis; after the subject of a composite nominal clause, pp. 115–21

יַצִּיבָא/יַצִּיב (5x)

HALOT, pp. 1892–93; *Holladay*, p. 408 (cf. מִן in *HALOT*, p. 1919)

ADVERB
1. what is certain, reliable, true, irrefutable (adjective)
2. מִן־יַצִּיב surely, as is certain [emphatic]
3. yes of course, certainly (positive, affirmative)

BDB – exclamatory; substantive, p. 1096
Rosenthal – [emphatic], p. 43 (§88)
Vogt – emphatic adjective, adverb, pp. 157–58

יָת (1x; Dan 3:12) (Heb. אֶת)

HALOT, p. 1894; *Holladay*, p. 408

INDIRECT OBJECT MARKER
   1. (a mark of the accusative) [c]

BDB – mark of accusative, p. 1096
Cook – direct object marking, p. 222 (§359b)
Rosenthal – preposition introducing the direct object,
   pp. 24, 41 (§§31, 84)
Vogt – sign of the accusative, p. 160

יַתִּיר (8x)

HALOT, p. 1895; *Holladay*, p. 408

ADVERB
   1. extraordinary [adjective]
   2. exceedingly [degree]

BDB – [degree], p. 1096
Cook – adjective used as an adverb of degree, p. 215 (§347c)
Rosenthal – [degree] p. 43 (§88)
Vogt – adjective; *adverb*: [degree], p. 161

כְּ (63x) (same in Heb.)

HALOT, p. 1896; *Holladay*, p. 408

ADVERB
   1. as (someone like) [resemblance] [1]
   2. compound expressions: כִּדְנָה (see further דְּנָה),
   כְּמָה and כַּחֲדָה (in contrast with, see further
   כְּעַן, כְּעֶנֶת, כְּעֶת) [4]

PREPOSITION
1. according to, corresponding with [in accordance with/according to] [2.a]
2. approximately, about [approximate quantities] [2.b]

CONJUNCTION
1. as soon as (with infinitive) [temporal] [3]
2. compound expressions: כְּדִי (see further דִי) [4]

BDB – [resemblance]; [in accordance with/according to]; [approximate quantities]; [temporal with infinitive], p. 1096

Cook – resemblance; identity; approximate quantities, pp. 123–24 (§181); temporal (with infinitive), p. 254 (§419)

Rosenthal – comparison; [identity]; [in accordance with/according to]; [approximate quantities]; temporal, p. 38 (§78)

Vogt – *preposition*: [resemblance]; [in accordance with/according to]; [temporal with infinitive]; *adverb*; emphatic, pp. 161–62

כְּדִי (5x) (Heb. כַּאֲשֶׁר)

see דִי in *HALOT*, p. 1851; *Holladay*, p. 402

CONJUNCTIONS
1. as (הֵא־כְדִי) [comparative] [3.f.α]
2. when [temporal] [3.f.α]

BDB – [comparative]; [temporal], p. 1088

Cook – manner, p. 253 (§416); temporal subordinator, p. 254 (§418)

Rosenthal – temporal, but tending occasionally toward a causal meaning, p. 42 (§86)

Vogt – [comparative]; [in accordance with/according to]; [temporal]; [purpose]; [result]; [nominalizing], pp. 163–65

כִּדְנָה (4x) (Heb. כָּזֶה ,כְּ/כָזֹאת)

see דְּנָה in *HALOT*, pp. 1854–55; *Holladay*, p. 402

ADVERB
   1. so, something like this, such a thing [manner] [3.α]

BDB – [manner], p. 1089
Cook – manner, pp. 217–18 (§351c)
Rosenthal – modal demonstrative adverb, p. 44 (§92)
Vogt – [manner], p. 165

כָּה (1x; Dan 7:28) (Heb. כֹּה)

HALOT, p. 1896; *Holladay*, p. 408

ADVERB
   1. עַד־כָּה as far as here, hitherto, up to this point
     [temporal]

BDB – [temporal], p. 1096
Cook – temporal adverb, p. 215 (§349)
Rosenthal – local demonstrative adverb, p. 44 (§91)
Vogt – [manner]; [temporal]; [locative], pp. 165–66

כַּחֲדָה (1x; Dan 2:35)

see חַד in *HALOT*, p. 1869; *Holladay*, p. 405

ADVERB
   1. together [manner] [e]

BDB – [manner], p. 1079
Cook – manner, p. 218 (§351d)

Rosenthal – modal assertive adverb, p. 44 (§94)
Vogt – [manner], p. 128

כְּלָה (1x; Dan 4:32)

see לָא in *HALOT*, p. 1906; *Holladay*, p. 410

ADVERB
1. כְּלָה חֲשִׁיבִין like people of no account [comparative negation] [2]

BDB – כְּלָה חֲשִׁיבִין as men not accounted of [comparative negation], p. 1098
Cook – לָא is used as a substantive: כְּלָה חֲשִׁיבִין considered as naught [comparative negation], p. 239 (§387d)
Rosenthal – כְּלָה חֲשִׁיבִין considered as naught [comparative negation], p. 43 (§87)
Vogt – כְּלָה חֲשִׁיבִין accounted as nothing, adverbial כְּ [comparative negation], pp. 188–89

כָּל־קֳבֵל דִּי (15x)

see קֳבֵל in *HALOT*, p. 1966; *Holladay*, p. 419

CONJUNCTION
1. forasmuch as, because [causal] [2]
• כָּל־קֳבֵל דְּנָה מִן־דִּי just because
2. although [concessive] [2]

BDB – [causal]; [concessive], p. 1110
Cook – causal; consequence; concessive, pp. 250–51 (§408); manner, p. 253 (§415b)
Rosenthal – [causal]; [concessive], p. 42 (§86)

Vogt – [causal]; [concessive], pp. 285–86

כָּל־קֳבֵל דְּנָה (7x)

see קֳבֵל in *HALOT*, p. 1966; *Holladay*, p. 419

CONJUNCTION
1. correspondingly, accordingly [in accordance with/according to] [2]
2. thereupon, then [logical consequence] [2]

BDB – [logical consequence], p. 1110
Cook – [logical consequence]; [in accordance with/according to], p. 136 (§200d)
Rosenthal – modal, p. 41 (§84)

כְּמָה (2x; both in Dan 3:33)

see מָה in *HALOT*, p. 1912; *Holladay*, p. 411

ADVERB
1. how! [exclamatory] [4.a]

BDB – [exclamatory], p. 1099
Cook – exclamations, p. 215 (§347d)
Rosenthal – modal demonstrative adverb, p. 44 (§92)
Vogt – [exclamatory], p. 198

כֵּן (8x) (same in Heb.)

HALOT, p. 1899; *Holladay*, p. 409

ADVERB
1. thus, so (always anticipatory) [manner]

BDB – [manner], p. 1097
Cook – manner, p. 217 (§351a)
Rosenthal – modal demonstrative adverb, p. 44 (§92)
Vogt – before direct discourse; comparative; before a
purpose or result clause; in adverbial expressions,
pp. 170–71

כְּנֵמָא (5x)

HALOT, p. 1899; Holladay, p. 409

ADVERB
1. thus, so [manner]
   • anticipatory with אמר, כתב
   • resumptive with עבד

BDB – [manner], p. 1097
Cook – manner, p. 217 (§351b)
Rosenthal – modal demonstrative adverb, p. 44 (§92)
Vogt – before indirect discourse; comparative, p. 172

כְּעֵן/כְּעַן (13x) (Heb. עֵת and עַתָּה)

HALOT, p. 1901; Holladay, p. 409

ADVERB
1. now (always at beginning of clause) (temporal)

BDB – [temporal], p. 1107
Cook – discourse marker, p. 261 (§430a)
Rosenthal – temporal demonstrative adverb, p. 44 (§89)
Vogt – [temporal]; [logical consequence]; introducing in a
letter, after the name of the addressee, the body of the
message [discourse marker], pp. 173–75

כְּעֶת/כְּעֶנֶת (4x) (Heb. וְעַתָּה)

HALOT, p. 1901; Holladay, p. 409

ADVERB

1. וּכְעֶת/וּכְעֶנֶת and now (like כְּעַן, it is rather a link into what is to follow, and marks the transition to the real point of concern in a letter) [temporal]

BDB – always in a letter, introducing the business of the letter, and to be connected with what follows, not, as MT, with what precedes, p. 1107

Cook – discourse marker; the verse-final placement of כְּעֶנֶת/כְּעַן in MT Ezra (4:10, 11, 17; 7:12) obscures the function of these particles, p. 261 (§430a)

Rosenthal – temporal demonstrative adverb, p. 44 (§89)

Vogt – introducing in a letter, after the name of the addressee, the body of the message [discourse marker], p. 174

לְ (378x) (same in Heb.)

HALOT, pp. 1904–6; Holladay, pp. 409–10

PREPOSITION

1. (direction or aim of movement) [directional] [1]
2. at the end of, for ever (temporal) [2]
3. as, for, (purpose) [3]
   - with הוה to become as
4. to, in order to (with infinitive after verbs of going, sending, saying, being able, etc.) [4]
5. with infinitive after לָא (prohibition) [5]
   - לָא לְהַשְׁנָיָה not to be changed
6. to, for, to tell to (with a personal object) [6]
   - at beginning of letters (without verb)
7. for (dative of advantage) [7]

8. belong to (meaning, to have) (dative of possession) [8]
9. (used to express other relationships) [9]
   • to resemble something
   • corresponding to
10. (as a periphrasis for the genitive) [10]
11. (in dates) [11]
12. (replaces accusative marker) [12]
13. (introduces emphatic apposition) [13]
14. (as an element in compound expressions) [14]
   • with קְבֵל, גּוֹא, מָה, עַד

BDB – after verbs of saying, declaring, writing, giving, offering, going, etc.; as mark of accusative; [product/stative]; [specification]; [possession]; as periphrastic for the genitive; purpose; [in accordance with/according to]; temporal; *with an infinitive*: after such verbs as be able, think, need, agree, command, decree; purpose; with לֵא, p. 1098

Cook – *noun complement*: marks the complement with verbs of transferring, the recipient of giving (indirect object), the addressee of speaking or informing, pp. 117–18, 208–10 (§§177a, b, 339); marks the direct object receiving the action of a transitive verb, pp. 118, 222 (§§177c, 359a); marks the goal or endpoint with verbs of motion, pp. 118, 203–4 (§§177d, 331); marks orientation or direction with verbs denoting stance, p. 119 (§177e); marks the possessor of a thing or trait in copular or existential clauses, pp. 119, 231, 234 (§§177f, 377b, 380d); indicates the product or final state with verbs of becoming or making, p. 119 (§177g); ethical dative, pp. 119, 207 (§§177h, 336); *prepositional phrases used adverbially*: advantage (or disadvantage); time; intended purpose; distribution by quantity or time, pp. 119–20 (§178a–d); periphrastic genitive, pp. 104,

120 (§§163, 178e); linking nouns in compound phrases, pp. 88, 120 (§§142b, 178e); plus infinitive marks either an infinitival complement pp. 121, 259–60 (§§178f, 428); or an adverbial clause (usually purpose), pp. 121, 247 (§§178f, 401); joined to lexical words or other prepositions to make further prepositions, p. 121 (§178g)

Rosenthal – every aspect of direction; local; temporal; modal; final; ownership; denotes indirect object and direct object; precedes the infinite in final clauses, pp. 38–39 (§79)

Vogt – *before a noun or pronoun*: for dative, after verb of giving, saying, etc.; לְ of the accusative; לְ of the genitive; possessive; interest or disinterest; ethical dative (giving emphasis); direction; place; temporal; purpose; varied uses; *before an infinitive*: purpose; after a verb of commanding, etc.; after other verbs; as a complement to a noun; as gerund, pp. 177–87

לָא (82x) (Heb. לֹא)

HALOT, p. 1906; *Holladay*, p. 410

NEGATIVE PARTICLE

1. (negating a clause) [1]
   - with דִּי and imperfect = lest, so that not
   - to express a prohibition
   - לָא אִיתַי (= Heb. אַיִן)
   - וְהֵן לָא and if not (used elliptically)
2. (negating a word) [2]
   - לָא בְחָכְמָה not because of
   - כְּלָה חֲשִׁיבִין like persons of no account
   - כָּל־מֶלֶךְ ... לָא no king
   - דִּי לָא without
   - דִּי לָא לְבַטָּלָא irrevocable; דִּי לָא הַשְׁנָבָיָה unlimited (with לְ and infinitive)

BDB – [negation]; with infinitive and לְ; with interrogative, p. 1098

Cook – negation, pp. 237–39 (§386); לָא with אִיתַי, pp. 233, 239 (§§380a, 387a); used modally with the infinitive, pp. 198, 239 (§§322, 387b); with interrogative particle, pp. 239, 240 (§§387c, 390b); substantival, p. 239 (§387d)

Rosenthal – negative statements; negation of individual parts of a sentence; substantival, p. 43 (§87)

Vogt – negating a clause; in negative purpose clauses; [as particle of non-existence]; negating a word; before preposition בְּ, pp. 187–89

לְגוֹא (6x) (Heb. גַּו II)

See גַּו in *HALOT*, p. 1843; *Holladay*, p. 401

PREPOSITION
  1. in, into [spatial] [b]

BDB – [spatial], p. 1086
Cook – [spatial], p. 121 (§178g)
Vogt – [spatial], p. 81

לָהֵן I (3x; Dan 2:6, 9; 4:24) (same in Heb.)

HALOT, p. 1907; *Holladay*, p. 410

CONJUNCTION
  1. therefore [logical consequence]

BDB – [logical consequence], p. 1099
Cook – introduces a sentence drawing a conclusion from the preceding discourse, p. 262 (§433)

Vogt – [logical consequence], p. 192

לָהֵן‎ II (7x)

HALOT, pp. 1907–8; *Holladay*, p. 410

CONJUNCTION
1. except, unless (as an introduction to a sentence) [exceptive] [1]
2. but, yet (adversative) [2]

BDB – [exceptive]; [adversative], p. 1099
Cook – exceptive quantifier; can serve as a discourse conjunction, indicating a fact contrary to expectation, or a limitation of a generality, p. 263 (§434)
Rosenthal – [adversative]; [exceptive], p. 42 (§85)
Vogt – conditional [concessive]; adversative, pp. 191–92

לְוָת‎ (1x; Ezra 4:12) (Heb. מֵעִם‎)

HALOT, p. 1908; *Holladay*, p. 410

PREPOSITION
1. near, beside (with מִן‎) [directional]
   • מִן־לְוָתָךְ‎ coming from you to here

BDB – [directional], p. 1099
Cook – directional, p. 134 (§197)
Rosenthal – [directional], p. 41 (§84)
Vogt – [directional], p. 193

לְמָא‎ (1x; Ezra 6:8)/לְמָה‎ (2x; Ezra 4:22; 7:23)

see מָה‎ in *HALOT*, p. 1912; *Holladay*, p. 411

CONJUNCTION
> **1.** for what purpose, lest [negative purpose] [B.4.b]
> • לְמָא דִי about what, on how

BDB – [negative purpose], p. 1099
Cook – negative purpose, p. 250 (§406)
Rosenthal – [negative purpose], p. 42 (§86)
Vogt – negative conjunction of purpose, p. 199

לְמָא דִי (1x; Ezra 6:8)

see מָה in *HALOT*, p. 1912; *Holladay*, p. 411

CONJUNCTION
> **1.** about what, on how [specification]

BDB – [specification], p. 1099

לְמַן־דִּי (4x)

see מַן in *HALOT*, p. 1918; *Holladay*, p. 412

RELATIVE PARTICLE
> **1.** to whomsoever [independent relative] [1]

BDB – [independent relative], p. 1100
Cook – indefinite pronoun ("light-headed" relative clause),
   pp. 95–96 (§151)
Rosenthal – indefinite relative pronoun, p. 26 (§37)
Vogt – indefinite relative pronoun, p. 208

לְקָבֵל (7x) (cf. Heb. נֶגֶד)

see קֳבֵל in *HALOT*, p. 1966; *Holladay*, p. 419

PREPOSITION

1. before, in front of, opposite (spatial) [1]
   - because of [causal]
   - הֵן . . . לָקֳבֵל דְּנָה if . . . then [conditional apodosis]
   - לָקֳבֵל דִּי just as [manner]

BDB – [spatial]; [reason/cause], p. 1110
Cook – [spatial]; [in accordance with/according to]; [causal],
   p. 135 (§200); לָקֳבֵל דִּי: manner, p. 253 (§415)
Rosenthal – [spatial]; modal, p. 41 (§84)
Vogt – *preposition*: [spatial]; [in accordance with/according
   to]; [causal]; *with conjunction* דִּי: [manner], pp. 284–85

לָקֳבֵל דְּנָה (1x; Ezra 4:16)

see קֳבֵל in *HALOT*, p. 1966; *Holladay*, p. 419

CONJUNCTION

1. הֵן . . . לָקֳבֵל דְּנָה if . . . then [conditional apodosis]

BDB – [conditional apodosis], p. 1110
Vogt – [conditional apodosis], p. 285

מָא/מָה (14x) (Heb. מָה)

HALOT, p. 1912; *Holladay*, p. 411

INTERROGATIVE/RELATIVE

1. what? (interrogative pronoun) [B.1]
2. what (= that which) (relative pronoun) [B.2]
3. מָא דִּי, מָה־דִּי [B.3]
4. (with a preposition) [B.4]
   a. כְמָה how! [exclamatory] [B.4.a]
   b. לְמָה lest [negative purpose] [B.4.b]
      - לְמָא דִּי on how [specification]

c. עַל־מָה why? [interrogative] [B.4.c]

BDB – [interrogative]; [indefinite relative]; with prefixes, p. 1099
Cook – indefinite pronoun ("light-headed" relative clause),
   pp. 95–96 (§151); quantifier, p. 113 (§170); interrogative,
   pp. 241–42 (§391b)
Rosenthal – indefinite relative; interrogative, p. 26 (§§37–38)
Vogt – interrogative pronoun; exclamatory adverb; indefinite relative pronoun; negative conjunction of purpose,
   pp. 198–99

מָה דִּי (6x) (Heb. מָה אֲשֶׁר, מִי אֲשֶׁר)

see דִּי in *HALOT*, p. 1851; *Holladay*, p. 402

RELATIVE PARTICLE
   1. that which [independent relative] [2.d]

BDB – [independent relative] p. 1087
Cook – indefinite pronoun ("light-headed" relative clause),
   pp. 95–96 (§151)
Rosenthal – [independent relative], p. 26
Vogt – indefinitive relative pronoun, pp. 198–99

מָן (מַן־) (10x) (Heb. II מָן)

HALOT, p. 1918; *Holladay*, p. 412

INTERROGATIVE/RELATIVE
   1. who? (interrogative pronoun) [1]
      • מַן־הוּא אֱלָהּ דִּי who is a god who = what god?
      • מַן אִנּוּן שְׁמָהָת who (= what) are the names?
   2. מַן־דִּי who, whomsoever (relative pronoun) [2]
      • לְמַן־דִּי to whomsoever

BDB – interrogative pronoun; [independent relative with דִּי],
   p. 1100
Cook – indefinite pronoun ("light-headed" relative clause),
   pp. 95–96 (§151); interrogative, pp. 240–41 (§391a)
Rosenthal – indefinite relative pronoun, p. 26 (§37); interrogative pronoun, p. 26 (§38)
Vogt – interrogative pronoun; indefinite relative pronoun, p. 208

מַן־דִּי (6x)

see מַן in *HALOT*, p. 1918; *Holladay*, p. 412

RELATIVE PARTICLE
   1. who, whomsoever [independent relative] [2]
      • לְמַן־דִּי to whomsoever

BDB – [independent relative], pp. 1087, 1100–1101
Cook – indefinite pronoun ("light-headed" relative clause),
   pp. 95–96 (§151)
Rosenthal – indefinite relative pronoun, p. 26 (§37)
Vogt – indefinite relative pronoun, p. 208

מִן (119x) (same in Heb.)

HALOT, pp. 1918–19; *Holladay*, p. 412

PREPOSITION
   1. (spatial) [1]
      a. out of, from, down from, away from [source] [1.a]
      b. (particular instances) [1.b]
         • מִן־יַד (deliver) from the hand of (abstract)
         • (judgment is executed) מִן = upon (him)
         • בְּעָה מִן to make a request from
   2. since (temporal) [2]

- מִקַּדְמַת דְּנָה formerly
3. different from, more than (comparative) [3]
4. from, of (partitive) [4]
   - מִן־נִצְבְּתָא something of (the hardness)
   - מִנְהוֹן ... וּמִנְהוֹן some of them ... others of them
   - מִן־קְצָת ... וּמִנַּהּ a bit of this ... and a bit of that
5. on account of, because of, as a consequence of
   (author/originator or reason/cause) [5]
6. according to, corresponding to, in fact [in
   accordance with/according to] [6]
   - מִן־יַצִּיב as is certain

BDB – place; source; immediate cause or result; remoter
cause or reason; norm; partitive; temporal; comparative;
compounds, p. 1100

Cook – point of origin; original state or location; perceiver;
cause; partitive; starting point; comparative, pp. 124–26
(§§182–184)

Rosenthal – local direction; temporal direction; partitive;
comparative, p. 39 (§80)

Vogt – separative; comparative; partitive; temporal; origin;
authorship; causal; specification; in a composite adverb,
pp. 208–14

מִן־אֱדָיִן (1x; Ezra 5:16) (Heb. מֵאָז)

see אֱדָיִן in *HALOT*, p. 1807; *Holladay*, p. 396

ADVERB
1. since, from that time on [temporal]

BDB – [temporal], p. 1078
Cook – temporal, p. 216 (§350a)
Vogt – [temporal], p. 25

מִן־גּוֹא (1x; Dan 3:26) (Heb. II גַּו)

see גַּו in *HALOT*, p. 1843; *Holladay*, p. 401

PREPOSITION
1. out, out from [source] [c]

BDB – [source], p. 1086
Vogt – [source], p. 81

מִן־דִּי (4x)

see דִּי in *HALOT*, p. 1851; *Holladay*, p. 402

CONJUNCTION
1. after, as soon as, insofar as [temporal] [3.f.β]
2. because [causal] [3.f.β]

BDB – [causal]; [temporal], p. 1088
Cook – causal, p. 252 (§410); temporal, p. 255 (§421)
Rosenthal – [temporal]; causal, p. 42 (§86)
Vogt – [temporal]; [causal], pp. 214–15

מִן־לְוָתָךְ (1x; Ezra 4:12) (Heb. מֵעִם)

see לְוָת in *HALOT*, p. 1908; *Holladay*, p. 410

PREPOSITION
1. coming from you to here [directional]

BDB – [directional], p. 1099
Cook – directional, p. 134 (§197)
Rosenthal – [directional], p. 41 (§84)
Vogt – [directional], p. 193

מִן־קֳדָם (11x)

see קֳדָם in *HALOT*, p. 1967; *Holladay*, p. 419

PREPOSITION
1. before [spatial] [3]
   • with דְּחָלִין to be afraid in God's presence
     (Heb. מִלִּפְנֵי) [metaphorical]
   • on the part of, from (Heb. מִפְּנֵי) [source]

BDB – [source]; [metaphorical], p. 1110
Cook – [source]; [spatial], p. 136 (§203d)
Rosenthal – [spatial], p. 41
Vogt – [source]; [metaphorical]; [agency]; [spatial], pp. 286–89

מִן־קְשֹׁט דִּי (1x; Dan 2:47)

see מִן in *HALOT*, p. 1919; *Holladay*, p. 412

CONJUNCTION
1. it is in accordance with the truth that, (meaning,
   indeed, truly), it corresponds to the truth that = in
   fact [in accordance with/according to] [6]

BDB – norm [in accordance with/according to], pp. 1088, 1101
Rosenthal – [in accordance with/according to], p. 39 (§80)
Vogt – [in accordance with/according to], p. 299

מִן־תְּחוֹת (2x; Jer 10:11; Dan 4:11)

see תְּחוֹת in *HALOT*, p. 2006; *Holladay*, p. 424

PREPOSITION
1. away from under [locative]

BDB – [locative], p. 1117
Vogt – [locative], p. 343

מִן־תַּמָּה (1x; Ezra 6:6)

HALOT, p. 2007; *Holladay*, p. 425

ADVERB
    1. from there [locative] [5]

BDB – [locative], p. 1118
Rosenthal – local demonstrative adverb, p. 44 (§91)
Vogt – [locative], p. 345

נֶגֶד (1x; Dan 6:11) (same in Heb.)

HALOT, p. 1926; *Holladay*, p. 413

PREPOSITION
    1. in the direction of, towards [directional]

BDB – [directional], p. 1102
Cook – [directional], p. 136 (§201)
Rosenthal – [directional], p. 41 (§84)
Vogt – [directional], p. 222

עַד (35x) (Heb. II עַד)

see עַד in *HALOT*, p. 1943; *Holladay*, p. 415

PREPOSITION
    1. up to [1]
        a. even to, thus far (spatial) [1.a]
            • as much as (quantitative)

b. until, until now, during, within, at last (temporal) [1.b]

CONJUNCTION
   1. until [temporal] [2]
      a. with imperfect [2.a]
      b. עַד דִּי with imperfect; with perfect [2.b]
         • לָא . . . עַד דִּי not . . . until = hardly, scarcely

BDB – *preposition:* space; amount; time; *conjunction:* of past time; of future, p. 1105

Cook – *preposition:* spatial limit (including figurative extensions); temporal limit; temporal extent; limit of amount, pp. 126–28 (§187); *conjunction:* temporal, pp. 254–55 (§420)

Rosenthal – temporal; local direction; modal; inclusive finality, p. 39 (§81)

Vogt – preposition: place and time; a space of time; conjunction: [temporal]; [purpose], pp. 245–46

עַד אָחֲרֵין (1x; Dan 4:5)

see עַד in *HALOT*, p. 1943; *Holladay*, p. 415

ADVERB
   1. at last (temporal) [1.b]

BDB – temporal, p. 1105
Rosenthal – temporal demonstrative adverb, p. 44 (§89)
Vogt – a space of time, p. 246

עַד־דִּבְרַת דִּי (1x; Dan 4:14)

see דִּבְרָה in *HALOT*, p. 1848; *Holladay*, p. 401

CONJUNCTION
   1. for the purpose of, so that [purpose]

BDB – [purpose], p. 1087
Cook – purpose, p. 249 (§404)
Rosenthal – [purpose], p. 42 (§86)
Vogt – [purpose], p. 86

עַד דִּי (12x)

see עַד in *HALOT*, p. 1943; *Holladay*, p. 415

CONJUNCTION
    1. until [temporal] [2.b]

BDB – temporal, p. 1105
Cook – temporal, pp. 254–55 (§420)
Rosenthal – [temporal], p. 42
Vogt – [temporal], p. 246

עַד־כָּה (1x; Dan 7:28) (Heb. כֹּה)

see כָּה in *HALOT*, p. 1896; *Holladay*, p. 408

ADVERB
    1. as far as here, hitherto, up to this point [temporal]

BDB – [temporal], p. 1096
Cook – temporal adverb, p. 215 (§349)
Rosenthal – local demonstrative adverb, p. 44 (§91)
Vogt – [manner]; [temporal]; [locative], pp. 165–66

עוֹד (1x; Dan 4:28) (same in Heb.)

HALOT, p. 1945; *Holladay*, p. 416

ADVERB

1. still [temporal]

BDB – still [temporal], p. 1105
Cook – time relative to another implied time, p. 216 (§350b)
Rosenthal – temporal assertive adverb, p. 44 (§90)
Vogt – [temporal], p. 248

עַל (104x) (same in Heb.)

HALOT, pp. 1946–47; *Holladay*, p. 416

PREPOSITION
    1. (up) on [locative] [D.1]
        a. at rest; on (one's neck) = around [D.1.a]
        b. on (to) [directional] [D.1.b]
    2. over, e.g., (appointed) over (the administration) [authority] [D.2]
        a. (with various verbs) [D.2.a]
        b. מְטָא עַל fall to (someone) [D.2.b]
    3. against [hostility] [D.3]
    4. towards (with verbs of motion) [directional] [D.4]
       • to [epistolary]
    5. (relating to the mind [perceptual] [D.5]
       • with שִׂים טְעֵם, and with שִׂים בָּל
       • (be pleasing) to (with לְ and infinitive)
    6. concerning, on behalf of, in this matter [specification] [D.6]
       • עַל־מָה why?
       • עַל־דְּנָה therefore [causal]
    7. above, more than (comparative) [D.7]

BDB – [locative]; [authority]; [spatial comparison]; [directional]: after a verb of motion, [hostility]; in various phrases, p. 1106

Cook – location; direction; change of posture; area of control; experiencer; beneficiary/maleficiary; additive; object of attention, pp. 128–30 (§188)

Rosenthal – locative; mental or modal application; direction; hostile direction; superior position; greater intensity, pp. 39–40 (§82)

Vogt – [locative]; [spatial]; authority; direction; [epistolary]; [perceptual]; [hostility]; [specification]; [causal]; [advantage]; [estimative]; expressing affect or emotion; [superlative], pp. 251–57

עֵלָּא (1x; Dan 6:3)

HALOT, p. 1947; *Holladay*, p. 416

PREPOSITION
1. עֵלָּא מִן over, above [metaphorical]

BDB – [metaphorical], p. 1106
Cook – [metaphorical], p. 216 (§349c)
Rosenthal – [metaphorical] (with comparative מִן), p. 39 (§80)
Vogt – [metaphorical], pp. 257–58

עַל־דִּבְרַת דִּי (1x; Dan 2:30)

see דִּבְרָה in *HALOT*, p. 1848; *Holladay*, p. 401

CONJUNCTION
1. for the purpose of, so that [purpose]

BDB – [purpose], p. 1087
Cook – purpose, p. 249 (§404)
Rosenthal – [purpose], p. 42 (§86)
Vogt – [purpose], pp. 85–86

עַל־דְּנָה (7x)

see עַל in *HALOT*, p. 1947; *Holladay*, p. 416

CONJUNCTION
1. therefore [logical consequence] [D.6]
   • in this matter [specification]

BDB – [specification]; *conjunction*: [logical consequence], p. 1089
Rosenthal – mental or modal application, p. 39 (§82)
Vogt – [logical consequence]; [specification], p. 101

עַל־מָה (1x; Dan 2:15)

see מָה in *HALOT*, p. 1912; *Holladay*, p. 411

INTERROGATIVE
1. why? [interrogative] [B.4.c]

BDB – interrogative, p. 1099
Cook – information seeking questions, p. 242 (§391b)
Vogt – interrogative, p. 198

עִם (22x) (same in Heb.)

HALOT, p. 1950; *Holladay*, p. 416

PREPOSITION
1. together with, (along) with, near (spatial) [1]
   • with מַלִּל speak with = to [declarative]
   • with עֲבַד (wonders he has done) with = toward; (what you shall do) with (someone) = treat someone [advantage]
2. עִם־לֵילְיָא by night (temporal) [2]

- עַם־דָּר וְדָר from generation to generation

BDB – [accompaniment]; [declarative]; [hostility]; temporal, p. 1107
Cook – accompaniment; benefactive action; temporal; reciprocal, pp. 131–32 (§189)
Rosenthal – [accompaniment]; temporal; [declarative]; [hostility]; [resemblance]; [relational], p. 40 (§83)
Vogt – [personal accompaniment]; [metaphorical]; [assistance]; [declarative]; [advantage]; [hostility]; [object accompaniment]; [additive], pp. 262–65

צְדָא (1x; Dan 3:14)

HALOT, p. 1963; *Holladay*, p. 418

ADVERB
1. הַצְדָא really, in truth; is it true that . . . ? [assertive question]

BDB – usually (malicious) purpose, p. 1109
Rosenthal – modal assertive adverb, p. 44 (§93)
Vogt – [assertive question], p. 281

קְבֵל (Heb. נֶגֶד) (29x)

HALOT, p. 1966; *Holladay*, p. 419

PREPOSITION
1. before, in front of, opposite (spatial) [1]
   - because of [causal]
   - הֵן . . . לָקֳבֵל דְּנָה if . . . then [conditional apodosis]
   - לָקֳבֵל דִּי just as [in accordance with/according to]
2. with כָּל־ [2]

- כָּל־קֳבֵל דְּנָה accordingly [in accordance with/according to]; thereupon, then [logical consequence]
- כָּל־קֳבֵל דִּי because [causal]; although [concessive]
- כָּל־קֳבֵל דְּנָה מִן־דִּי just because [causal]

BDB – substantive; spatial; causal; with כָּל: causal; concessive, p. 1110

Cook – [spatial], p. 135 (§200a)

Rosenthal – directional; modal, p. 41 (§84); with כָּל: causal; concessive, p. 42 (§86)

Vogt – [spatial]; [in accordance with/according to]; [causal]; with דִּי, pp. 284–86

קֳדָם (42x)

HALOT, p. 1967; Holladay, p. 419

PREPOSITION
1. before (temporal) [1]
2. before, in front of, in the sight of (spatial) [2]
   - in the sight of [estimative]
3. מִן־קֳדָם before [3]
   - with דָּחֲלִין to be afraid in God's presence (Heb. מִלִּפְנֵי) [metaphorical]
   - on the part of, from (Heb. מִפְּנֵי) [source]

BDB – locative; temporal; with מִן, p. 1110

Cook – [spatial]; temporal, with מִן, p. 136 (§203)

Rosenthal – locative, temporal; as an honorific preposition with nouns that signify gods, kings, or others of high rank; with מִן, p. 41 (§84)

Vogt – [locative]; temporal; after a verb of saying, etc.; after a verb of motion; after other verbs; [estimative]; with מִן, pp. 286–89

שַׂגִּיא (13x) (same as Heb.)

HALOT, p. 1985; *Holladay*, p. 421

ADVERB
1. great [adjective] [1]
2. much, many (with singular collective) [adjective] [2]
3. very much, very [degree] [3]

BDB – adjective; *adverb*: [degree], p. 1113
Cook – adjective used as an adverb of degree, p. 214 (§347a)
Rosenthal – [degree], p. 43 (§88)
Vogt – adjective; *adverb*: [degree], pp. 311–12

תְּחוֹת (5x) (Heb. תַּחַת)

HALOT, pp. 2005–6; *Holladay*, p. 424

PREPOSITION
1. under [locative]
   • with מִן away from under

BDB – [locative], p. 1117
Cook – locative, p. 138 (§205)
Rosenthal – [locative], p. 41 (§84)
Vogt – [locative], p. 343

תַּמָּה (4x) (Heb. שָׁם, שָׁמָּה)

HALOT, p. 2007; *Holladay*, p. 425

ADVERB
1. there [locative] [5]
   • מִן־תַּמָּה from there
   • דִּי . . . תַּמָּה where

BDB – [locative], p. 1118
Cook – lexical adverb, p. 215 (§349a)
Rosenthal – local demonstrative adverb, p. 44 (§91)
Vogt – [locative], p. 345

תְּנְיָנוּת (1x; Dan 2:7)

HALOT, p. 2008; *Holladay,* p. 425

ADVERB
  1. for the second time, once again [repetition]

BDB – [repetition], p. 1118
Cook – [repetition], p. 217 (§350f)
Rosenthal – [repetition], p. 43 (§88)
Vogt – [repetition], p. 346